You Are My Witnesses:

Drawing from Your Spiritual Journey to Evangelize Your Neighbors

Charles Van Engen

WIPF & STOCK · Eugene, Oregon

Wipf and Stock Publishers
199 W 8th Ave, Suite 3
Eugene, OR 97401

You Are My Witnesses
Drawing from Your Spiritual Journey to Evangelize Your Neighbors
By Van Engen, Charles

ISBN 13: 978-1-60899-047-4
Publication date 9/3/2009
Previously published by Reformed Church Press, 1992

Contents

Foreword

The reason the Christian church exists, according to Acts, is to be Christ's witnesses. This is how Jesus described the purpose and the promise of that community from which he departed on the mount of the ascension (Acts 1). The coming of the Spirit would bring it about: out of the disciples' doubt and confusion would emerge the faithful witness of a company of forgiven and empowered sinners, who would carry the good news of God's love in Christ to Jerusalem, Judea, Samaria, and to the ends of the earth (vs. 8). "Evangelization" (the saying of the gospel to bring about the response of faith) was to be the church's central purpose, and "witness" would define Christian identity.

The expansion of the Christian church in the first several centuries of its history was the demonstration of the Spirit's empowerment in action. In some way or another, as historians of mission show us, the church has always been involved in the evangelistic mission given it by Christ. We may sometimes have valid doubts about the methods used, and we will constantly question the ways in which the gospel has been adapted and reduced as it has entered one culture after another. But the fact is that the church has always understood its purpose to be making the gospel known. This purpose has not been called "evangelism" until fairly recently in the church's history, but the term still addresses the original mission or apostolate of the church: to be Christ's witnesses.

Evangelism, both the word and the activity, has fallen on hard times in America in the latter half of the twentieth century. The excesses of the electronic church and entrepreneurial evangelists contribute to the prejudices many Americans already have about the term and the activities known as evangelism. For these and other reasons, the mainline Protestant churches have become more and more wary of it. For many, the term evangelism evokes negative associations of manipulation, hard-sell, insensitive pressure, and emotionalism. It has gone so far that, in the view of one African missiologist knowledgeable about the American scene, Christians in this country "have lost their nerve" when it comes to the church's evangelistic mission.

This loss of nerve parallels the loss of members in many Protestant denominations and the growth of many independent churches and movements. We may rejoice that many of these movements are reaching people with the message of Christ, but at the same time we must ask questions about the definition of the gospel which is often being proclaimed. How often is the evangelism which "works" in America based on a gospel which fits too neatly into the American value system: success, prosperity, well-being, happiness? Is *all* the gospel, whose witnesses we are to be, *always* being communicated? Or, is it being tamed and conformed to make its success more certain? That concern on the part of many of the more traditional Christian churches tempers their enthusiasm for evangelism. We are uncertain about how to go about it, perhaps even about what evangelism is. But we are sure that we cannot in good conscience make those compromises which appear to be needed in order to be "successful."

This is not a new problem. If we read the earliest New Testament literature carefully, we can see that abuses of evangelism were already there from the beginning. When Paul, in the second chapter of 2 Thessalonians, states that he and his colleagues did not resort to "deceit or impure motives or trickery" (vs. 3) when they evangelized the Thessalonians, he is implying that this was, in fact, happening. In defending their way of doing evangelism, Paul emphasizes that they proclaimed "the gospel of God" (vs. 2) even though it was often opposed. He stresses that they did not seek to please their hearers or to make their message attractive: their concern was solely to please God. That meant that the way they evangelized had to be in harmony with the content of the gospel. Thus, he compares their approach to that of a gentle nurse, and even goes so far as to say that they were "determined to share with you *not only* the gospel of God but also our own selves, because you have become so very dear to us" (vs. 8). I never cease to wonder at the boldness of that "not only," linked to "the gospel of God." It is a truly amazing emphasis upon the integrity which must be inherent in our Christian witness!

This commitment to evangelization which witnesses to the whole gospel and which does so in ways which express that good news is found in Charles Van Engen's *You Are My Witnesses*. Dr. Van Engen emphasizes that it takes time and work to grapple with all that the gospel is and means for us in our world today. There are many misconceptions and dilutions of the gospel which we encounter, and which we very possibly bring with us. There is great pressure on us to make the gospel witness pleasing and effective, rather than faithful to our Lord and to his purposes. How can we know that our witness is truly pleasing to God? That confidence can emerge only out of our own focused encounter with God's Word. There can be no biblically responsible evangelistic witness apart from disciplined study of Scripture linked with constant prayer. Those who carry out this witness will be people who are themselves experiencing the gospel in new ways and being evangelized as they study, pray, and discuss.

In the chapters which follow, we are invited to experience this gospel and prepare for its witness by studying the second chapter of Acts. As we do this, we move from Pentecost to the formation of the first Christian community in Jerusalem. The encounter with this text takes us to the heart of the church's calling. It emphasizes our dependence upon God's empowering presence in our midst. It stresses that the gospel is intended to enter into every person's life individually AND to form believers into a witnessing community. It challenges us to ask: Why are we not that kind of community today? What will it take for us to become such a community?

As the participants in this study move through it, they will constantly discover that evangelistic witness is not really an individual activity; it is a work of the Christian community, expressed through each of its members. The original promise Christ gives the church in Acts 1.8 is plural in this address, and the title of this book is also plural: You *are* my witnesses. This means that Jesus' mandate is given to the community and is to be carried out by the community, which the Spirit has been empowering for this task since Pentecost. Evangelistic witness emerges from the shared experience of the love of God in Christ and the exploration of the gospel which happens when Christians are gathered together. This is what Acts 2 (and the remainder of Luke's book) so clearly teaches.

This evangelistic ministry does not happen automatically or spontaneously. It is the result of decisional preparation, of willingness of believers to embark upon this adventure of spiritual growth. All Christians are witnesses, whether they choose to be or not; the question is whether they are useful, responsible witnesses, a community through which the good news of God's love does flow and reach out to others. It takes the decisions of believers, the commitment to grow in faith and to deepen one's understanding of the gospel, for redemptive witness to take place. It is helpful that Dr. Van Engen has not merely written a book *about* witness, but has instead written a book which guides the *study* and *doing* of witness. For it to be fruitful, this study will need to be undertaken with seriousness and purposefulness. Its strength is in its insistence that Christians become intentional about their witness.

The purpose of evangelism is the saying and demonstrating of God's good news so that people will be brought to faith and become a part of the company of witnesses, the church. The great tendency in America to treat faith as private and individual must be countered. This book provides a way to do that as it invites individuals to become an intentional faith community, to allow their own stories with God to be shared and to be used by God's Spirit to equip others for witness. It takes courage to embark upon this experience, but it is the courage which God's spirit provides and which the Christian needs in order to grow in Christ. The point of our evangelistic witness is not to make the church bigger, but to respond to Christ's loving command and to experience the fulfillment of the promise that we will be his witnesses! God's work through the church is ultimately for the benefit of all of creation. After all, John emphasized that "God so loved the *world* that he sent his son. . ." (3.16).

Clearly, it is a difficult time to do evangelism. But we have no choice; we must be about the task of Christian witness if we are to be faithful to our calling! Charles Van Engen has done a signal service for congregations who decide to embark upon the study of Christian evangelism which is presented in this book. *You Are My Witnesses* will enable the serious preparation of Christian women and men for their evangelistic ministry, and it does so where it belongs: in the congregation. The congregation which carries out this study will experience the gospel in new ways, both internally and externally. No one can move through this particular adventure and remain unchanged. That is, however, the essence of growing faith: constant discovery of more of God's love in Christ, more of the gospel, more of what it is that God will accomplish in us and through us.

Darrell L. Guder
William A. Benfield, Jr. Professor of Evangelism and Global Mission
Louisville Presbyterian Theological Seminary

Preface

We know that at least 80 percent of all new church members become part of a local congregation because of a previous relationship or friendship with another member of that congregation. Yet in spite of a number of excellent books written concerning relational evangelism, little seems to happen in actually motivating, training, and mobilizing our church members to evangelize their neighbors, friends, business associates, and family members. A more common pattern is for pastors and church leaders to hold classes concerning evangelism and then to drop the subject before the members can begin to evangelize their acquaintances.

The most appropriate, natural, and effective evangelists in North America today are the average church members who have understood their own faith journey, become open and sensitive to the faith-hunger of those around them, tapped into their own pilgrimage for evangelistic material, and learned to share the gospel in a manner that is appropriate to their neighbors.

This book seeks to get beyond the normal routine of most evangelism approaches that endlessly train church members for evangelism but seldom involve them in actually evangelizing. It is written as an action-reflection training manual to be used by small groups in local churches, led by a facilitator who is also involved in evangelizing a neighbor, friend, or acquaintance.

The book is designed for use by a small group that will meet for about three hours each week for ten weeks. There are, however, a number of ways this material can be used.[1] Each member of the group will select an acquaintance with whom that member will seek to witness in a sensitive, listening, relational manner. Preparation for such witness will involve prayer, personal spiritual growth, informed reflection, sensitive preparation, and careful cultivation of a meaningful friendship with the person's "neighbor," on that person's terms. The book will stimulate the group's reflection upon, mutual support for, and intentional sensitivity to, each member's commitment to witness to one other person during the ten weeks of the seminar.

A recent survey of Reformed Church in America pastors demonstrated that they consider evangelism to be the number one priority in their congregations.[2] But the declining membership of almost all mainline denominations points to the lack of strong, dynamic, and effective evangelization on the part of local churches. Pastors and people need to discover new ways to evangelize the unchurched in North America.

The primary audience of this book consists of members of local congregations in North America who are themselves Christian, who accept the Bible as God's Word for today, and who are excited enough about their faith to want to share it with others.

There has been a phenomenal proliferation of books on evangelism during the last fifteen years. Many of these make significant contributions to the field. A number of approaches specifically designed for congregational use have also been offered. Examples include: *Good News People* (Reformed Church in America), *Evangelism Explosion* (James Kennedy), *Night of Caring / Night of Sharing* (Paul Cedar), *Evangelism Primer* and the *Friend-Maker Resources* (Ben Johnson), *A Place to Dig In—Doing Evangelism in the Local Church* (William Hinson), and *A Church's Guide to Evangelism* (Richard Peace). All of these resources are well done and have been used to good effect in some places.

The basic material of this book has been taught a number of times as a seminary course in relational evangelism and differs in several respects from other works in the field. First, this book is based on a view of evangelism laid out in Acts 2. The outline of the book follows the development of the Acts 2 pattern. Second, it teaches church members to draw from their own faith pilgrimages for sharing their faith in a natural, effortless, and non-threatening way. They will learn to "console those who are in any affliction with the consolation with which we ourselves are consoled by God" (2 Cor. 1.4).

Third, this book draws cross-cultural communication theory from literature in church growth and evangelism, from James Fowler's faith stages, and from literature in the theology of conversion. This book will integrate these various areas of thought in terms of evangelizing our neighbors. The process is designed to help church members find ways of intentionally praying for those with whom they have natural, ongoing relationships, sensitively listening to them, wisely communicating their message in an appropriate manner, and clearly understanding how the Spirit works in their lives. This book follows an action-reflection format, calling on church members to begin the seminar by prayerfully selecting a person with whom to share their faith, then walking them through the entire process of evangelism, as seen in the outline.

The book begins by calling for open discussion of each participant's basic attitudes and understanding of evangelism. Subsequent chapters follow a clearly defined process that begins with the exposition of the appropriate passage in Acts 2. Each chapter proceeds to a reflection on the theme of that chapter, to an illustration of it in everyday life, to a group discussion of related issues, and finally to appropriate action. The participants are taught to derive their specific action steps from their careful and intentional reflection on what God wants to do, on their own faith pilgrimage, and on the day-to-day unfolding of the life and needs of their "neighbor."

[1] If the members of your evangelism group are not able to commit themselves to ten three-hour sessions, some other options might include the following:

a. Meet for two hours each week for fifteen weeks. After the organizational meeting you might ask the members to read the first chapter for information. The first regular meeting would then be spent getting acquainted and praying together, as per the "Discussion" and "Action" parts at the end of Chapter One. From then on, the members could read each chapter at home. The discussion time could be shortened each week, leaving adequate time for prayer. Please do not shorten the prayer time! It is crucial!

b. Meet for one hour each week (say, during the regular Sunday school hour) for twenty weeks. In this case, your group could cover each chapter in two weeks. One week the members would read the material at home and engage in the "Discussion" of its substance during their hour together. The next week would involve the "Action" section, including prayer time, with reference to the previous week's material.

Actually, almost any schedule of meetings would be appropriate. Whatever the schedule, the meetings should be held on a regular basis, without long delays between sessions. If too much time goes by without the members of the group seeing each other, they will not be able to keep up with what the Holy Spirit is doing in their lives and, through them, in the lives of their neighbors. It is important that your group find a comfortable and workable schedule, because that makes it easier for the members to covenant together and to commit themselves to attend as regularly as possible. Continuity and regularity are essential for the members as they pilgrimage together and share their faith journeys.

[2] Corwin Smidt and James Penning, "Priorities for the Church," The *Church Herald* (XLVII: 8, August 1990), pp. 20-23.

CHAPTER ONE

Understanding Evangelism in the North American Context[1]

If you are a member of a Christian church in North America and have demonstrated your interest in evangelism by enrolling in a study group aimed at teaching you how you may evangelize your neighbor—then this book is for you. But the book is intended to be only a starter, a stimulus to discussion in your evangelism group, and a catalyst to new discoveries as you learn to naturally, sensitively, and creatively witness to your neighbor from the wellspring of your own spiritual pilgrimage.

Your interest in evangelism calls for you to be aware of the peculiar nature, obstacles, and opportunities of doing evangelism in North America. Many evangelists and missiologists consider North America to be one of the most difficult places in the world to do evangelism. We who live here all the time often cannot see the difficulties facing us, just as someone who lives in the forest often loses awareness of the trees. Sometimes we need to hear from those who come to us from outside our own North American culture. They can help us understand more deeply and clearly what we are facing when we join together to evangelize North America. I have been tremendously enriched by their observations, so I pass some of them on to you.

EXPOSITION

Several years ago the pastors and elders of the Presbytery of Chiapas came to say farewell. They represented some of the fastest-growing churches in the world. The president of presbytery presented my wife and myself with a gift and words of appreciation for our work with them. "Go now as missionaries sent by the National Presbyterian Church of Mexico to the church in the United States. We understand that for some time now our sister churches in North America have not been growing in their membership. Go to them for us, and teach them how to evangelize their country the way we have learned to do it here."

The words of his commission have stayed with me. The circle is being completed, and we in North America can now profit from the perspectives and advice of our brothers and sisters from the Third World. They can give us insight and urgency for bringing the gospel to our people in a new and exciting way. So let's begin with some observations, acknowledge the obstacles, make a note of the opportunities, and set ourselves some objectives for evangelizing North America.

OBSERVATIONS

Members of churches in Africa, Asia, and Latin America find it perplexing to see that evangelism in North America is presently not a high priority for most North American Christians—and in fact has been the neglected child of much of mainline Protestantism during the past several decades. They find it hard to understand how the mainline denominations who have been their historic mothers, sisters, and now ecclesiastical partners have consistently declining membership. They wonder why, when we have been able to help them evangelize their parts of the world, we cannot impact our own culture for the gospel. Most perplexed are those Third World Christians who labor under tremendous pressure from other religions, severe restrictions in their evangelistic activities, and radical shortages of personnel, materials, and finances. As a pastor from India once asked me, "How is it that with such liberty, wealth, and popular openness to the Christian religion, many Christian churches in North America are not evangelizing their people?"

Although many of us tend to think of ours as a "Christian" nation, others looking in see the beam in our eye because it is so obviously similar to phenomena they encounter in their own contexts. These issues help us understand that our evangelistic task is really one of "evangelizing neo-pagan North America," as Al Krass has put it.[2] Lesslie Newbigin recently reminded us that if we take the gospel seriously in all of its biblical breadth, we find it radically questioning some of the most basic presuppositions of our culture.[3] Although at the outset we might consider the evangelization of North America a simple task, on more careful consideration we will find significant obstacles which make our context very difficult to impact with the claims of Jesus Christ.

OBSTACLES

In this chapter we will highlight only a few of the obstacles most often identified by Third World Christians as being especially true of our situation in North America. These tend to fall into two major categories: obstacles in our culture and obstacles in our churches.

Obstacles in Our Culture

There are certain built-in obstructions in our cultural setting which must be squarely faced and overcome in order for the gospel to impact North America. Here we will mention only three.

No need for help from God

I remember crossing the U.S.-Mexico border once, accompanied by my family and two Mexican women. We were on our way to a large convention of Christian women to be held in the northern part of the United States. The two women were from Chiapas, Mexico, and had been very active in evangelism over several decades. As we rode through the luxurious cities and countryside of southern Texas, one of them commented, "It appears that these people don't need God." I asked her what she meant. She responded that, compared with their own situation—in which people deal daily with the presence of extreme poverty, the lack of physical safety, constant job insecurity, uncertainties regarding housing and food, daily family crises, and a general lack of control over their own destiny—the people of North America don't appear to need God. Insurance companies take care of accidents and other crises, workers' compensation cares for the unemployed, and school systems look after nearly everyone's basic education. In short, health, welfare, and the pursuit of happiness are given secular answers—though, in fact, they entail spiritual questions.

As we rode, we talked more. The second woman went on to observe, "It appears that in this culture there is no space for God." People appear busy with family, work, recreation, social life, and the personal pursuit of wealth. Where, then, is there space for God?

Since seeing our culture through their eyes, I have carefully taken note of the arenas of life mentioned during congregational prayer times. Is it not true that our need for God is narrowed to matters of health and personal crisis—with a political or global issue thrown in once in a while? Whole arenas of life like food, clothing, housing, education, work, recreation, social relationships, finances, and personal moral choices—matters which are commonly subjects of prayer in other cultures—are seldom mentioned in our own prayer times. Even less are they considered to be religious issues in our North American culture. No wonder we seem rather tongue-tied and embarrassed when we begin to talk about God. Our culture pushes us to speak of religious faith and commitment as something separate from the daily life of the people of North America. But a careful reading of Scripture teaches us a different reality. God in Jesus Christ through the Spirit is interested in permeating all arenas and transforming every aspect of our lives.

No need for public faith

Issues of faith have also been separated from public life. Once, while attending an ecumenical consultation in New York City, I spoke with an Arab Christian who emphasized this to me. "In the Middle East our religious affiliation is a public matter, highly visible, politically significant, and publicly demonstrated. Islam forces us in that direction. Though that creates severe religious, social, and political tensions, I sometimes think it is easier to deal with than this culture, where in terms of public demonstration you cannot guess the religious affiliation of many of the people around you."

What a different perspective from that of my friend Dirk, a milkman from Monnickendam, the Netherlands! As I sat in his living room I listened to him expound at length on how religious faith and religious affiliation are matters of taste and personal preference. Influenced strongly by a Western world view, Dirk showed me two bottles of wine, one white and one red. "Some people like white wine, others like red," Dirk explained. "You like Reformed Christianity, my brother Hans likes the Seventh Day Adventists, I like no religion at all. You see, each individual should be free to choose whatever is his or her personal preference, and we will respect each other's choice."

This "live-and-let-live" thinking seems to be regarded highly in our North American culture. People inside and outside the church give strong support to a notion of tolerance that essentially squeezes faith-language out of public life altogether.

But this is a contradiction of the very heart of the gospel which speaks of one God who created all people; one Jesus Christ with authority over all creation at whose name every knee shall one day bow; and one Spirit who convicts the world of sin, righteousness, and judgment. (See Matthew 28, Colossians 1, Romans 5 and 6, Philippians 2, and John 16.8.)

The reduction of religious faith to individual and private spheres of personal preference is a major obstacle to evangelization in North America. Particularly strong in the older, culture-affirming denominations, it robs us of the vitality and urgency of communicating the gospel in our context. Our desperate fear of anything that smells of "propaganda" and "proselytism" is a direct result of narrowing religious issues to matters of private taste. Other religious movements in our midst seem to have no such fear. We who worship the God of the universe and Jesus Christ in whom all things subsist need to overcome our fear of publicly demonstrating our faith.

No need for radical conversion

A third obstacle is even more pervasive and subtle. A non-Christian medical doctor in Tapachula, Chiapas, Mexico, who had done extensive study in the United States, mentioned this issue to me. He spoke of the fact that in the United States people seem to be constantly bombarded by religious literature and by radio and television programs. He then referred to the law of diminishing returns and of deafness caused by too much noise, of blindness caused by too much light. "I believe," he said, "that religious overkill in the U.S. has produced similar reactions on a personal and spiritual plane." He was pointing to a very significant obstacle resulting to some extent from our own evangelistic and revivalist history.

Turn on your radio or television on Sunday morning. You are bombarded by evangelist preachers. Study the general population of the "unchurched" in North America and you discover that their contact with the church has been quite extensive—but mostly negative. Many have once gone forward in an evangelism crusade and possibly even signed a decision card. But they have little personal faith and seldom attend church. Many of the unchurched, in fact, have quite good and understandable reasons why they essentially have given up on the church. As O'Connell and Gallup have observed:

> We boast Christianity as our faith, but many of us have not bothered to learn the basic biblical facts about this religion. Many of us dutifully attend church, but this act in itself appears to have made us no less likely than our unchurched brethren to engage in unethical behavior.
>
> We say we are Christians, but sometimes we do not show much love toward those who do not share our particular religious perspective. We say we rejoice in the good news that Jesus brought, but we are often strangely reluctant to share the gospel with others. . . .
>
> We say we are BELIEVERS, but perhaps we are only ASSENTERS.[4]

Obstacles in Our Churches

In evangelizing North America, we need to be aware of obstacles found in our churches. Here we will highlight two which deal with a basic lack of clarity in defining our task and understanding our faith.

Our task is unclear

A couple of years ago a pastor from Taiwan emphasized the fact that, in his perception, North Americans do not seem to know what the word evangelism means. He questioned how we can speak about evangelizing North America without having a clear definition of what the task is. I think his question is important. One of our greatest internal obstacles during the last several decades seems to be our lack of clarity in defining evangelism.

Our uncertainty about what evangelism is has contributed to strong negative images on the part of the members of our churches. During the past several years I have had the opportunity of asking pastors and seminary students to describe their feelings, impressions, and memories conjured up by the word evangelism. Their responses have been overwhelmingly negative. Images of manipulative techniques, of decision cards never followed up, of door-to-door intruders, of sidewalk confrontations, and of ranting television and radio evangelists have produced strong negative reactions. But I have also found that when these same people are helped to get beyond their negative images and to gain a positive and biblical view of evangelism, they become overwhelmingly participatory and active.

Our faith is unclear

A few years ago the Rev. Jorge Lopez, a pastor in the National Presbyterian Church of Mexico, spent several quarters living in Western Michigan and attending a seminary there. Upon his return to Chiapas, he commented that he found our church members to be weak in their knowledge of the Bible, uncommitted to the church's programs, and passive in their evangelistic outreach. At first I thought his critique rather severe. But the last few years have taught me otherwise. We seem to be suffering from a kind of biblical anorexia. My dictionary tells me that anorexia is a "loss of appetite," often due to prolonged periods of not eating properly. Our biblical illiteracy is a major obstacle to our being used as God's instruments for evangelizing our neighbors.

It is an accepted fact in evangelism that you cannot share what you do not have. Lack of clarity in matters of Scripture and faith produces a lack of enthusiasm for, and a real avoidance of, personally sharing our faith. Our reluctance to participate in evangelism is obvious. Few pastors of North American churches consider their primary calling to be evangelizing the unchurched, and few members view sharing their faith to be their major spiritual activity. A look at our congregational budgets readily illustrates the low priority assigned to evangelism. Staff salaries, building maintenance, and programs for members themselves far outweigh the amount of time, effort, and money allocated for evangelism. Major congregational programs like Bethel Bible Study and Stephen's Ministries are targeted primarily for present church members rather than for the unreached. Kenneth Chafin, a Southern Baptist pastor and dean of the Billy Graham School of Evangelism, put it bluntly: "The average congregation has little meaningful contact with those who are not Christian."[5] It seems that concern for the preservation of our history, traditions, and church life obscure our commitment to the fact that "God so loved the *world* (it does not say 'the church') that he gave his one and only son" (John 3.16).

The obstacles we have noted above are not new, nor are they insurmountable. Rather, they can teach us that effective evangelism is neither magic nor miraculous—but just plain hard work. The obstacles demonstrate the urgency of maximizing the potential provided by magnificent opportunities for evangelism in the North American context. Nowhere in the world are such opportunities so readily available to local congregations as they are in North America. Nowhere are there greater possibilities for impacting a culture with the gospel.

OPPORTUNITIES

Christians from the Third World often remark about the fantastic range of evangelistic resources available to us in North America. These opportunities may be found both in the culture at large as well as in the church.

Positive Cultural Receptivity

In 1985 Robert Bellah and his associates published a very significant study which pointed to the essential role of Christianity in American culture. Basing their research on a massive five-year study of various American communities, the authors conclude that Americans, largely confined to a vocabulary of individualism, have lost the language needed to make moral sense of their lives.[6] Yet Bellah and his associates concluded that personal faith in its various expressions is essential for North American society and is sought by many as a source of meaning in their lives.

The study done by the Schuller Ministries and the Gallup Organization which we noted earlier also points to the incredible potential of evangelism in North America:

> The prospect for deepening America's spiritual commitment is far from hopeless. Virtually all Americans are, in some measure, drawn to the person of Jesus Christ. . . . Many believe he is the Son of God, and even many among the nondevout feel that Jesus' life and person tell us something profound about the meaning of existence. And, remarkably, as many as nine in ten

> say that Jesus as a moral and ethical leader has had at least some impact on their lives.
>
> Furthermore, at least half of Americans wish their religious faith were stronger, and a perhaps surprising one fifth of non-believers say they would like to believe in the divinity of Jesus Christ. . . .
>
> A remarkable four in ten Americans have an intuitive or experiential basis for their belief and report a dramatic religious experience. . . . And seven in ten of all survey respondents feel that their relationship with Jesus Christ is deepening.[7]

Christians in Third World countries do not have this kind of positive cultural background for evangelism. On the contrary, invariably their contexts call for radical encounter with other faiths which do not accept belief in Jesus Christ. Why are we not capitalizing on such remarkable receptivity?

Freedom, Finances, and Forms for Mass Evangelism

The general cultural receptivity looks even brighter when we consider the freedom of proclamation found in North America, coupled with the freedom of individuals to change their faith. Add to this the money, people, and programs available to us for Christian literature, mass media, videos, and so forth—and the possibilities skyrocket. The multimillions handled by television evangelists are not only a scandal. They also demonstrate the fantastic potential open to evangelists, pastors, and churches who wish to impact North America for Jesus Christ.

Compare that with a little radio program in Tapachula, Chiapas, Mexico. For a couple of years we were able to have a half-hour program of Christian music and a brief sermon for which I sometimes was invited to preach. What a tremendous amount of energy it took for Pascual, the brother in charge of the program, to gather the necessary money and people to do that half-hour program! Then came the fateful day when the radio station told Pascual that the Mexican government had decreed that no radio stations in Mexico would again be allowed to broadcast religious programs. All Protestant radio broadcasts were silenced that day and were not resumed until very recently. How well I remember Pascual lamenting the fact that the freedoms and resources available to Christians on the U.S. side of the border were not available to him on his side of the border. "What couldn't we do here if we had the resources and freedom available to Christians in the U.S.!" he exclaimed.

Myriad Relational Bridges

In the midst of such general cultural receptivity and potential resources, a third major opportunity is being emphasized by evangelists in North America. In every community one can determine where lies a given congregation's target population. It is to be found in the thousands of close and casual, formal and informal, personal relationships which church members have with the unchurched in the community. It does not take much work to find the businesses, recreational arenas, neighborhoods, schools, and networks of friendships impacted by the members of a congregation. Here are the most fruitful bridges for evangelizing North America. It is a proven fact that over 80 percent of all new church members originally came to the church because of previous friendship with a member of that congregation. Here, then, are the networks through which the gospel can be communicated naturally, lovingly, openly, personally, and effectively. We need to maximize the potential of our natural relationships.

Research, Data, Consultation, and Training

A pastor from Kenya was recently one of my students. He had been in the United States only a short time. One of his most telling comments had to do with the research and consulting resources which North American churches have to aid them in evangelism. "If we only had usable data to know who lives where in our country, how many there are, what needs they have, and how we can serve them! If we had such data I'm sure our church would be growing ten times faster than it is." As far as I know, his church is growing by about 30 percent each year because the members share their faith with their people! I wonder what their growth rate would be if the pastor in fact had the kind of data he desired!

We have those kinds of resources at our fingertips. Church consulting and training groups like the Alban Institute, the American Institute of Church Growth, the Yokefellow Institute, the Fuller Evangelistic Association, and the Billy Graham Schools of Evangelism are there to be tapped for consultation and research. Evangelism resources like those mentioned in the preface to this volume are but a few of the many approaches available to churches. Discipleship Ministries, led by the Rev. David Bruininks, and based in Holland, Michigan, is specifically designed to train the church's membership in discipleship and personal evangelism. The late Rev. Robert Bast, minister for evangelism and church development in the Reformed Church in America, launched "On the Way" (the approach for which this book was written), a long-term effort designed to equip congregations committed to evangelism and growth. There is no reason why a congregation that wants to evangelize North America cannot do so.

OBJECTIVES

The gap between personal faith and church attendance which we observed earlier can be bridged only by Christians in local congregations who embody the presence and love of Christ in that place. After all is said and done, Christ addressed no one else but his disciples when he said, "YOU will be my witnesses" (Acts 1.8; emphasis mine).

Christians from the Third World can do more than help us understand and analyze—they can also exhort and challenge. The fantastic growth of the church in China under incredible oppression and seemingly insurmountable odds calls all of us to reexamine our methods and our commitments. The explosive growth of churches in Africa challenges the effectiveness of our own response to the opportunities before us. The rapid growth of base ecclesial communities, of Pentecostal fellowships, and of suffering Protestant churches in Latin America serves as an example to us of the tremendous effect which vibrant, Spirit-filled and Spirit-led churches can have on their society.

The churches of North America stand in need of drawing sap from their roots and receiving sustenance from the evangelical and revivalist foundations of their history. Third World Christians, in their exhortations to North American churches, have stressed the importance of renewal. We are called to heed what Paul said to the Corinthian church: that we need to become "new creations" in Christ, to be reconciled to God through Jesus, to be called to the "ministry of reconciliation," and to participate actively in Christ's work of "reconciling the world to himself." This re*NEW*al of ourselves empowers us to be, then, "ambassadors for Christ, since God is making his appeal through us." This involves us in a revolutionary movement of radical transformation! "[God] made him to be sin who had no sin, so that in him we might become the RIGHTEOUSNESS OF GOD!" (2 Cor. 5.17-21; emphasis mine).

This newness begins by calling us to NEW PURPOSE. It reminds us that the purpose of the church, its reason for being, is not to preserve a tradition, to maintain a building, to serve its members, or to pay the bills. The church's purpose is to be the covenant people of God who seek the reconciliation of all persons with God and with each other, so that through the church, "all the families of the earth shall be blessed" (Gen. 12.3).

This newness involves a NEW HEART—a heart of compassion and love which yearns deeply for the transformation of the world and for the coming of the Kingdom of God. This love is the heart of the gospel and the central essence of the body of Christ (Jer. 31; John 14). This is the heart that seeks to be God's instrument (ambassador, servant) in the world for Jesus' sake through the power of the Spirit.

Newness entails a NEW URGENCY which will not rest as long as there are people who have not been impacted by the gospel. It is the sense of being "debtors"—that we *owe* it to the people of the world to present them the gospel. The urgency comes from understanding that the world will not hear without a preacher, and the preachers will not proclaim unless they be sent—and it is in the SENDING that we find our true nature as the people of God (Rom. 1.14-15, 10.14-15).

Newness calls for NEW APPROACHES and NEW METHODS. As someone once asked, "If the church is for everyone, why is not everyone in the church?" Do we believe that the gospel of Jesus Christ is really good news? The holistic perspective embodied in the gospel can make a major contribution to North American society. But are we sure of that? Do we feel that what we have to offer is as precious as a "treasure hidden in a field" (Matt. 13.44)? Can we believe that "there is no other name under heaven . . . by which we must be saved" (Acts 4.12)? If our answer is positive, we will constantly search for the most effective means by which we may carry out our calling to a ministry of reconciliation.

Finally, newness means a NEW CONVERSION. Lesslie Newbigin speaks of a three-fold conversion—conversion to God, conversion to the church, and conversion to the world. The evangelization of North America calls us to a new examination of our own conversion. For many of us the process of conversion has been short-circuited. Recent discoveries concerning spirituality, like James Fowler's *Stages of Faith* and Henri Nouwen's works, are voices joined to those of the Third World calling us to a radical three-fold conversion to God, to church, and to the world for whom Christ died.

The evangelization of North America is not optional—it is the reason we exist. It is commanded by our Lord, and it is urgently needed for the sake of righteousness and reconciliation. What a marvelous gift from God! Our participation in God's mission makes us instruments through whom the "families of the earth" may be blessed. In the final analysis, evangelism is people sharing with people the love and grace of God in the power of the Holy Spirit. Third World Christians live this out in marvelous ways under severe pressures. Already more than half of all Christians live in Asia, Africa, and Latin America. Many predict that by the year 2000 the percentage of Christians on those continents will have risen dramatically, while the percentage of Christians in Europe and North America will have dwindled even further. I wonder if there is a way of responding to and offsetting those predictions?

I am still pursuing the commission given me by my Mexican brothers and sisters. Can we in North America learn enough from Christians in the Third World to reverse the trends? Will we allow them to challenge us to evangelize our neo-pagan continent? Third World Christians labor against tremendous economic, social, political, and religious odds, and they still continue to grow in the evangelization of their people. Can we do less? Will we let them help us? I wonder.

REFLECTION

1. This first chapter is offered to you as a stimulus for reflection and discussion. If you are part of a small study group, please take a few moments to answer the questions that follow. They may help you reflect further on what you have read. For your own record, you may want to write your answers in the space provided. If you do so, you can consult them again at the end of this study.

a. Describe the images, feelings, concepts, impressions, and memories which the word "evangelism" conjures up for you.

b. Describe the place, practice, and perception of evangelism in your congregation.

c. Write down how many non-Christians/unchurched people have been incorporated into your local congregation during the past year. Explain why they joined your church. Tell us if any of those new persons have shared their experience of an encounter with God.

d. Tell about the last time you wrote your personal faith pilgrimage. Tell if that pilgrimage was shared with another person—when, how, and with whom that happened, and what it was like.

e. Name and describe someone you know who would benefit from hearing about the way God has impacted your life.

f. Write the goal of evangelism in one sentence.

g. Write a one-sentence summary of the gospel as GOOD NEWS for the people of North America.

h. What does the word conversion mean to you?

DISCUSSION

1. It is important that the members of your evangelism task force begin to know each other and feel comfortable with each other. Take some time now for each one to give a little background about themselves to the rest of the group. Although they may feel they know each other well because they have seen each other at church for some time, there is probably something about each person that others in the group don't know. The leader may suggest that each person take this opportunity to tell something about themselves that may be of interest to the group. THE LEADER SHOULD MAKE CERTAIN THAT EVERYONE IN THE GROUP KNOWS EVERYONE ELSE'S NAME.

2. After all members of the group have had a chance to introduce themselves, the study group may want to spend time discussing some of the relevant material in this first chapter, as well as some of their answers to the questions. Especially important is to offer an opportunity for all participants to voice their negative images, frustrations, and concerns regarding evangelism in North America. Participants may also be encouraged to talk about obstacles and

opportunities that go beyond the material in Chapter One. What were your feelings about evangelism before reading this chapter? If your feelings were negative, was there an emphasis in this chapter that helped you feel more at ease about, and open to, evangelism?

ACTION

1. Commitment to Prayer

It has been demonstrated time and again that evangelization does not happen unless it is surrounded by prayer. The next ten weeks will be ones of exciting new discoveries for the members of the group. And for some of the members those discoveries may be related to some very deep issues in their own spiritual journey.

For that reason one of the components of this study program is that EACH MEMBER OF THE GROUP WILL COMMIT HIM/ HERSELF TO FIFTEEN MINUTES OF DAILY PRAYER FOR THE OTHER PERSONS IN THE GROUP FOR THE FOLLOWING TEN WEEKS. The leader should call for such a commitment, not asking for any manifestation of it on the part of the members, but requesting that they seriously consider this commitment and allow the Holy Spirit to give them the discipline and the desire to fulfill this commitment.

2. Praying together

At this point I suggest that the members of the study group gather in groups of two or three for at least fifteen minutes of prayer.

Pray for each other, as you begin this discovery class in learning to witness to your neighbor.

Pray for the people of North America, specifically mentioning persons who illustrate some of the issues that have been discussed.

Pray for your congregation, for its evangelistic vision and for its desire to incorporate new people.

Pray for the leader of your evangelism study group, for his or her own relationship with God.

Pray that the Holy Spirit will stimulate the people of the group to discover new ways the Spirit can use them to witness to their neighbors.

Pray for the leaders of your congregation, that the Spirit may give them the sense of urgency and deep commitment to do whatever is necessary to gather into your church those who as yet do not have a vibrant and transformational relationship with Jesus Christ.

Pray for the people of the area surrounding your congregation, that they may become "faith-hungry," open to the work of the Holy Spirit in their lives, and willing to listen to the word of the gospel through the lives and words of the members of your congregation.

[1] Most of the material in this chapter first appeared in *Reformed Review* (41:1, Fall 1987), pp. 9-20; reprinted in the *Journal of the*

Academy for Evangelism (Vol. 4, 1988-1989), pp. 45-55, and used by permission.

[2] Alfred Krass, *Evangelizing Neo-Pagan North America* (Scottdale: Herald Press, 1982).

[3] Lesslie Newbigin, *Foolishness to the Greeks: The Gospel and Western Culture* (Grand Rapids: Eerdmans, 1986).

[4] George Gallup and George O'Connell, *Who do Americans Say that I Am?* (Philadelphia: Westminster, 1986), pp. 88-89 (emphasis theirs).

[5] Kenneth Chafin, "Evangelism and the Local Church;" in Sherwood E. Wirt, edit., *Evangelism: The Next Ten Years* (Waco: Word, 1978), p. 120.

[6] Robert Bellah, Richard Madsen, William Sullivan, Ann Swidler, and Steven Tipton, *Habits of the Heart: Individualism and Commitment in American Life* (New York: Harper & Row, 1985).

[7] Gallup and O'Connell, op.cit., p. 89. The late Robert Bast, who served as the Reformed Church in America's minister for evangelism and church development, also noted these incredibly positive observations in his newsletter on evangelism, *Good News*, August, 1987.

CHAPTER TWO

Getting in Touch with Your Faith Journey

(Acts 2.1-4)

If evangelism is to be something more than religious propaganda or institutional proselytism, it must be biblical. It must be intimately related to God's free, gracious call to individuals to be reconciled to God, to each other, to their world, and to themselves (2 Cor. 5.11-21). In other words, we must make sure that our evangelism is God's work, not ours. William Abraham is right when he says that the bottom line in evangelism is initiating people into the kingdom of God.[1]

This emphasis is also important because there are so many varied techniques, schemes, and styles of evangelism presently being tried in North America. Yet much that passes for evangelism and ministry has little long-term impact. In fact, in the last fifteen years the percentage of church attenders in this country has not changed—ranging from 40 to 42 percent—in spite of tremendous efforts being expended through a multitude of approaches. This book focuses on one of the most basic problems facing Christians who want to reach out and touch North American people for Christ. Here we will concentrate on a common component of all the various evangelism efforts; we will study an essential aspect of all effective evangelism.

Sometime, someplace, somehow in all evangelism activities there must be a sharing of faith between the Christian and the non-Christian in such a way that the non-Christian is confronted with the possibility of a faith-encounter with Jesus Christ—an encounter that includes incorporation into the body of Christ, the church.

So this book, and your evangelism group's use of it, has the ultimate purpose of finding natural, non-manipulative, loving, and effective means for just such a personal encounter. It involves a process through which you may discover how to be a witness. You will find out how to share your faith-experiences with another person in such a way that your non-Christian neighbor may feel free to consider the possibility of being encountered by Jesus Christ through the operation of the Holy Spirit.

No matter what programmatic structure is followed to bring us to this point, sooner or later every evangelistic endeavor succeeds or fails precisely here. Faith-sharing is so important because, as we will learn, the inquirer (whom we are calling our "neighbor") receives our communication and determines whether faith-sharing will happen or not. Thus, the most effective evangelization will measure all approaches and processes from the perspective of the *listener*.

EXPOSITION

We have said that true Christian evangelism, if it is to be something other than propaganda or proselytism, must be biblical. In this book we will follow the earliest pattern of relational witness we find in the New Testament. It is the model followed by the apostle Paul, and one by which the church expanded throughout the entire Roman world. Luke carefully describes this New Testament approach in the second chapter of Acts.

Please take a moment now to read Acts 2.1-47. Luke does not develop the events of Acts 2 as an evangelism program to be carried out for a few months and then scrapped. This is not a technique or a series of videos provided by the evangelism specialist to a few interested members of the church. Rather, Luke presents a description of the lifestyle of a witnessing Christian community and shows us the *continuous process* through which the people of God may witness to their neighbors. We do not have space here to develop a complete Bible study of the passage, something your evangelism group may wish to do on its own. But let me highlight some of its most outstanding features. Notice the flow of the witnessing process as Luke describes it.

1. The disciples *experience* the presence of God in their lives through the coming of the Holy Spirit. This new spiritual experience is so powerful that they are immediately propelled out into the streets of Jerusalem to tell their story (2.1-4).

2. The neighbors (those people from all the nations surrounding Jerusalem who had come for the Jewish Passover feasts) begin to *ask questions*, and some are ready to listen (2.5-13).

3. Peter *listens* to the opinions expressed by the hearers and responds appropriately (2.14-15).

4. Peter *develops* a message (the kerygma, the gospel proclama-

tion) specifically designed for the agendas and concerns of his hearers (2.16-36).

5. The Holy Spirit *applies* the message and brings about a desire for conversion in the hearts of the hearers (2.37).

6. Peter gives these hearers *concrete and tangible means of expressing their conversion* (2.38-40).

7. Those who are converted are *immediately received* into the fellowship of the believers (2.41-42).

8. All the believers, new and old, *serve each other* in a communal lifestyle of mutual love, caring, and sharing (2.43-45).

9. All the believers, new and old, are *witnesses of their faith to the people around them* (2.46-47a).

10. *More new members are added* in a continuous reenactment of the pentecostal pattern (2.47b).

We know that North America of the 1990s is a radically different context than first-century Jerusalem. We are well aware that we cannot simply reproduce in our day what existed then. However, I believe Luke offers us a process which is Spirit-inspired and God-directed, a pattern that can be adapted, modified, and put to good use in any cultural or historical context. So let's begin.

REFLECTION

Acts chapter one tells us that Jesus commanded his disciples to "wait (in Jerusalem) for the gift (the Holy Spirit) my Father promised, which you have heard me speak about" (1.4, NIV). They were to wait until their spiritual experience included transformation through an experience of the presence of God by the Holy Spirit. To be witnesses, they needed to have something about which to witness. Their own encounter with God was prior to their witness. Luke wants us to remember that. In other words, the first step in Christian witness is getting in touch with our own spiritual autobiography.

Once again, please read Acts 1.4-6, 12-14; 2.1-4.

Please notice three very important issues highlighted by Luke in this story. First, the disciples of Jesus—men and women—were *together*, seeking God's presence in a corporate way. Throughout the Old Testament, God's presence was most often and most strongly discernible in the midst of God's people: the corporate cohesion of all those who professed allegiance to Israel's God and united themselves with those who considered themselves God's people. Pentecost comes not so much to separate, autonomous, independent individuals as it comes to God's people, gathered to share together their experiences of God's presence in their midst.

Second, notice that the disciples—men and women—were *devoting themselves to prayer*. We have yet to understand fully, to appreciate completely, the real impact which prayer had in the event of Pentecost—and the impact it may have in the events of your church's new pilgrimage in evangelism. In this manual we have built in a significant amount of time and intentionality for the practice of prayer because it is such an important part of the Pentecost paradigm of evangelism. In 1.14, 2.42, 4.31, 6.4, and 12.12 we see an emerging pattern. God's presence, the witness of the disciples, the powerful acts of God, and the resulting conversion of several thousand people are all events wrapped in a blanket of prayer. In Luke's account, the early disciples quite clearly believed that there was an intimate link between their life of prayer and the amazing events in which they were participating. This is clearly a call to you and me as well. Our path of discovery in relational evangelism is lined with places of prayer. Every step we take along that path needs to be accompanied and surrounded by prayer. If we learn anything together during these weeks, let's learn to pray.

Third, I want you to notice that while they were together, each person experienced the Spirit's transforming presence in an individual way. "All of them were filled with the Holy Spirit" (2.4). All the people there—women and men—were changed by their experience of God's presence—so changed that they clearly had something very important to talk about. In other words, they were *witnesses* because of the *experience* which was theirs in that room at Pentecost.

Paul was not there. He was a late-comer, one "untimely born." Paul encountered the resurrected Jesus Christ on the road to Damascus and in that *experience* was radically transformed. His transformation was confirmed and sealed by the Holy Spirit through Ananias' ministry of reconciliation, proclamation, and baptim (Acts 9.1-19). Interestingly, just like the other disciples, Paul immediately became a *witness* of his experience, one who had something to tell, and felt compelled to tell it (Acts 9.20-22, 27-31). In fact, all of Paul's sermons recorded in Acts are contextually adapted renditions of the same story—the story of Paul's encounter with Jesus Christ.

These elements of the Acts 2 process of relational evangelism are extremely important for us to understand today. In North America during the last twenty years or so there has been a major shift in the way persons will accept religious truth. There has been a shift away from the intellectual, propositional, and confessional understanding of religious truth. Today, non-Christian persons tend to be much more accepting of a strongly intuitive, emotive, and experiential kind of religious truth. They will often consider our experience as "real," but think of our many propositions and confessional statements as mostly irrelevant.

This shift has had a major impact on North American church life, and particularly on the evangelistic process. Although we apparently are seeing a major religious awakening in our country, much of that new awareness is being captured by New Age, by non-Christian religions, by spiritists, and even by the demonic. The primary reason for this is the experiential and existential basis of truth so prevalent in people's minds today. The pattern of relational witness in Acts 2 serves to point us to a faith-sharing process that is based on the historic truth about Jesus Christ, but which may be communicated in an existential, intuitive, and personal fashion acceptable and understandable to non-Christians in North America. After all, our stories, our *witness*, is not all that different from that of Peter, Mary Magdalene, Paul, or Priscilla.

Said negatively, you cannot share with another what you don't have yourself. Said positively, effective Christian witness in North America will draw from the depths of the wells of our own spiritual journeys and connect with the experiences of our neighbors in communicating God's love for them. Christians who want to witness today need to be aware of their own spiritual journeys.

A fourth aspect of Luke's story is its emphasis on the role of the members of the church. I have encountered in many churches a prevailing assumption that the pastoral staff is to be responsible for the congregation's evangelism program—if indeed there is one at all. But the members of the pastoral staff of a church are the *last* people we should look to for evangelism as a process of relational witness. In fact, the clergy are often so "ghettoized," so completely involved with those who are already Christians, that they are not in a position to participate in relational witness. The only exceptions I have encountered are clergy who intentionally involve themselves with "unchurchly" groups or tasks. They may be volunteer firefighters or may help in a local school or in local community services. They may intentionally make efforts to relate to their unchurched neighbors. Yet even those efforts may be misread by the non-Christian as attempts on the clergy's part to add them to their list of church members. The clergy's time is usually so taken up with churchly matters that the clergy are not naturally positioned for good relational witness. It is the *members* who are uniquely qualified for relational witness.

Now at this point we need to make a distinction. We find in Acts that Luke is talking about a process that involves *all* the members of the believing community. Later Paul will talk about the gifts of the Spirit, one of which is the gift of evangelism. In Acts 2 we learn a pattern of relational witness—not about the gift of evangelism. ALL CHRISTIANS ARE TO BE WITNESSES. There are *some* members (often just a few in each congregation) who seem to have the gift of evangelism. They can be recognized because of their facility in bringing people to Christ. Often they have a complementary gift, that of discernment. Often you will find that the Holy Spirit just keeps bringing new people to them, people who very quickly and naturally are converted through their ministry. Some of those with the gift of evangelism become mass evangelists, preachers, and church planters.

But in this book we are not dealing with that group of people—and you should not normally expect that you would have the gift of evangelism. In fact, I find too many people who shy away from evangelism precisely because they believe that either the clergy or someone with some kind of mysterious gift should do it. Luke's perspective frees us from such misconceptions. *Every Christian is expected to be a witness.* Here is where Luke's pattern is so helpful. You and I as members of the church are not necessarily expected to be preachers, teachers, theologians, or gifted evangelists. We should know our Bibles and we must know the essence of the gospel—but we do not have to be biblical scholars. We are called to witness to God's grace as that grace has taken place in our own individual lives—nothing more, nothing less. In other words, it is out of the depths of the well of our own spiritual journeys, out of our individual experience of the presence of God, that we will witness.

So we need to learn something about our spiritual journeys. At this point the work of Delos Miles may be helpful. In his *Introduction to Evangelism*, Miles gives some excellent suggestions regarding the use of spiritual autobiography in evangelism.[2] "The spiritual autobiography is your firsthand religious experience as it relates to the gospel story," Miles says:

> Think of your life story as one bolt of cloth. Like a cloth bolt, it has a beginning and an ending. Yet, all that is in-between is still the same cloth. It may wind and twist, flow and cling, but it's still the same cloth. So it is with one's life story. The entire life is but one bolt of cloth even if it is refashioned, recycled, and colored anew. Then, too, follow the threads in that bolt of cloth. See how intricately they are woven. Our lives have many threads running through them. As our story interfaces and intersects with God's story, all of these threads are pulled together into an harmonious whole. . . .
>
> Autobiography has been enlisted in the service of evangelism from the earliest days of Christian history. There has always been, and will always be, a prominent place for autobiography in the witness of the church.
>
> It is an effective way to tell the gospel story because it communicates with authority, variety, and interest from an incarnational stance. You are more believable than someone from the distant past.[3]

Delos Miles then goes on to suggest four very important guidelines for the use of autobiography in relational evangelism:

1. Autobiography should exalt God above all else and glorify him

above all others. . . . The purpose of autobiography is not personal glory, but the glory of God.

2. (Spiritual autobiography) should be intimate knowledge of God, religious experience which is firsthand, knowledge of God which is mediated through one's own [senses].

3. It should be capable of being communicated through varied forms of media. . . . Many Christians have used their journals and diaries to tell of their experiences with God. In John Wesley's journals we read about his heartwarming experience on Aldersgate Street. In George Whitefield's journals we read of his conversion experience. . . . A host of Christian witnesses have chosen to communicate their testimony to God's transforming grace in full-scaled autobiographies.

4. A fourth guideline for using autobiography in the service of evangelism is to remember that such data will be more effective when used with those who come out of one's own cultural context.[4]

I believe the Apostle Paul was thinking precisely of this use of spiritual autobiography when he wrote to the Christians in Corinth, "Praise be to the God and Father of our Lord Jesus Christ, the Father of compassion and the God of all comfort, who comforts us in all our troubles, so that we can comfort those in any trouble with the comfort we ourselves have received from God" (2 Cor. 1.3-4, NIV).

There are two ways to discover the real depth of comfort that is represented by the well of your own experiences with God. The first method is to begin to reconstruct your own story. However, your interest here is not so much in where you were, who you were with, or what happened to you. Rather, your interest is in asking deeper questions: When and where did I experience the presence of God? How did I recognize that God was there?

I believe that if you begin to reconstruct your own story, working backward from the present, you will discover that your pilgrimage has been a series of moments when you experienced God's presence in surprising, unexpected, and sometimes unsought ways.

This leads us to the second way you may discover God's presence in your spiritual autobiography. Rather than thinking of your entire journey, focus on a particular moment, a certain decision time, or a major turning point in your life. Ask again, Was God there? How was God working? Can I now see God in that event in a way I could not see at the time? Whom did God use as catalysts for me to hear God's voice? How did I respond?

By way of illustration, and following Delos Miles' guidelines, let me offer you a story from my pilgrimage. Some years ago I was vacationing in Michigan when a friend saw me hobbling about and insisted that I see his orthopedic surgeon. I could barely walk. Upon examining my knees, this Christian surgeon told me that he could not believe how I could stand the pain. He was not sure if my knees could be fixed. In fact, he wondered if I would ever walk again except with artificial knees. I was thirty-five years old, and my knees were about ninety-five years old. In fact, my knees were so bad that this particular surgeon did not want to work on them. Instead, he offered to send me to Lansing, Michigan, to the person from whom he had learned arthroscopic surgery.

Five months later I was in Lansing being worked on by another Christian surgeon who asked my wife and me to pray with him before the surgery. "I can scrape around in there and clean it out," he said, "but only God can heal you."

Well, I had known pain, but nothing like what I experienced after that surgery. The surgeons operated on both knees at once so I could recuperate faster, and for a number of days after the surgery I felt like someone had driven a truck over my legs. But it wasn't only the pain. The fear of not walking again; the sense of losing my masculinity, my strength, and my unlimited energy; the desperate longing to be whole again; and the long years of pain all came together in that event.

The third day after my surgery was Sunday. I encouraged my family to go to church that morning, and they left me sitting in a recliner chair in our house in Holland, Michigan, my legs propped up with big ice packs on my knees.

No sooner had I been left alone than a deep depression took hold of me. I began crying like a baby. "God, I can't stand this pain!" I shouted. "God, I have far too much to do, and too many people are expecting so much from me. I can't be sitting here like this!" Little did I know that I would sit in a wheelchair for the next several weeks and walk with a cane for the next sixteen months! "God, where are you?"

I turned on the television set and absentmindedly poked at the remote control to change the channels. Robert Schuller was ending a Sunday morning sermon. He was preaching a series of sermons on Job to highlight the new sculpture of Job that had been donated to his church. I heard him read a phrase from Job 23.10 (NIV): "But he knows the way that I take; when he has tested me, I will come forth as gold."

It was almost like someone was shouting it at me. As I write, eight years later, I still shiver at the words. I shouted them at the ceiling, "I will come forth as gold!"

I don't know what Schuller said about those words. But looking at the televised picture of the Job statue and shouting those words were part of one of my most complete, transformational, and cleansing experiences of God's presence. I felt God in the room. I felt God pouring his love and grace over my head, running down my shoulders, inundating me with the Holy Spirit. I could hear God's gentle whisper, "Believe me, after the experience of the cross, I too know what pain is."

I felt warmth in my knees and a beginning hope of relief from the ache in them. But much, much more than that, I knew beyond the shadow of a doubt that God is, that God loved me, that God was wrapping me in an envelope of care and comfort—and that I would "come forth as gold." I have on numerous occasions told this story to others who are in extreme physical pain, and they often find comfort in it. Sometimes they experience a clear and direct sense of God's care and comfort as well.

DISCUSSION

The members of your evangelism group may be invited at this point to take time to look back at their own spiritual pilgrimage. I suggest that the group take no more than fifteen minutes for personal, silent reflection. I encourage the group to then organize itself into pairs and to give members the opportunity to tell stories out of their own pilgrimages when they were certain God was present in their lives.

Two cautions are in order:

1. If anyone feels awkward telling a story from their spiritual journey, THEY SHOULD FEEL FREE NOT TO PARTICIPATE. There should be no pressure whatsoever on anyone who feels hesitant at this point. However, we should also remember that if we find it difficult or impossible to tell our story *within* the church, it may be that much harder with non-Christians.

2. Before people begin telling their stories to each other, the group should review the guidelines offered by Delos Miles, as they are given above. These are very important. It is crucial that the guidelines inform the way our stories are told.

ACTION

I suggest two parts to the action segment of this chapter.

1. Prayer

Have the group gather together again. Spend at least thirty minutes in prayer as a group. This time the prayers should be prayers of THANKSGIVING, thanking God for the experiences that have been shared by members of the group. Thank God for God's presence and provision in the lives of the ones who shared their stories with you. Briefly retell one of the stories in your prayer, and thank God for all the various details of the story. Tell God how much this story has been able to encourage you in your own spiritual pilgrimage.

2. The Spiritual Autobiography

The members of your evangelism group may wish to devote at least one hour between meetings to reconstruct, reflect on, pray about, and fill in various aspects of their spiritual autobiographies. The more they begin to learn about God's grace in their own lives, the better prepared they will be to *witness* about that grace.

[1] See William Abraham, *The Logic of Evangelism* (Grand Rapids: Eerdmans, 1989), pp. 13-14.

[2] Delos Miles, *Introduction to Evangelism* (Nashville: Broadman, 1983), pp. 161-176. Miles suggests Jeremiah 9.23-24 and 1 Corinthians 1.26-31 as helpful Bible readings at this point.

[3] *Ibid*, pp. 161-163.

[4] *Ibid*, pp. 163-166.

CHAPTER THREE

Encountering Your Neighbor to Whom You May Witness

(Acts 2.5-13)

A few years ago Corwin Smidt and James Penning, professors of political science at Calvin College in Grand Rapids, Michigan, surveyed 580 Reformed Church in America pastors. As part of a larger study, they asked the pastors to prioritize six tasks in which the church might be engaged: charity to individuals in need, work for social change to overcome injustice and oppression, guidance and counseling for individuals needing help, work for Christian moral standards nationally, evangelism overseas, and evangelism in North America. Their findings are significant for the study we are engaged in here. Although some of the responders categorized themselves as "mainline," while others called themselves either "evangelical" or both, the overwhelming priority emphasized by all of those surveyed was *evangelism in North America*. Seventy-two percent of the mainline pastors and 86 percent of the evangelical clergy placed evangelism in North America as their number one priority.[1]

If evangelism in North America is such an overwhelming priority in the minds of clergy, why are our churches doing so poorly in this area? If clergy really believe in evangelism, why do the membership figures of most mainline churches continue to decline every year? Clearly, there are a number of ways to answer these questions, and a whole range of issues is involved. In this chapter we will highlight only one of them. One reason for the membership decline in mainline

Protestantism may be that we do not listen compassionately and interact intentionally and sensitively with our neighbors when it comes to issues of faith. At this point please turn to the back of this book and read "A Parable of Fishless Fishermen" (Appendix A). Is a person a fisherman if year after year he or she never catches a fish?

The number of evangelism approaches attempted over the last several decades is staggering. The number of church members who have been trained in Evangelism Explosion and other methods is truly amazing. Yet, if one looks at the statistics of mainline church membership during the past twenty years, it would seem that little has come of all that energy, time, and personal commitment. Maybe one of the reasons behind such little success is that we have not been paying enough attention to the fish—we have not actually gone fishing. In other words, maybe we have forgotten to look for, understand, gather with, and listen to the people whom we hope to evangelize. Evangelism efforts that do not in fact evangelize the unchurched are a waste of time. What matters is not the kind of program your church might have. What matters is if people are coming to know Jesus Christ because someone in your church is being used by the Holy Spirit in their evangelization. Too often we are so concerned with HOW to do evangelism and with WHAT our message will be that we forget those who are the most important part of the process—THE HEARERS. The book of Acts forcefully demonstrates that the disciples were asking the right questions. After Pentecost they exploded out into the street. And their first question was not what to do or how to do it; their first task was to *listen* to the people.

EXPOSITION

Please read Acts 2.5-13. Luke dramatically reorients the narrative here. Having focused on the disciples, Luke suddenly directs our attention to the potential hearers of the gospel (vs. 5). He carefully describes them for us. In Chapter Four we will study more deeply how to understand and listen to our neighbors. What we want to stress in this chapter is that we must focus our attention on and make ourselves available to our neighbors.

Notice how Luke develops his narrative theology at this point. Who are these hearers? First, they are "devout Jews" (vs. 5), meaning that they were converts to the Jewish faith who were present in Jerusalem because of the festivities going on at the time. They were probably not all ethnically Jewish, but religiously they accepted the Jewish faith. Later, Paul would discover that this same group of people, the "devout" ones, would be the most receptive to the gospel in the synagogues which he would visit on his missionary journeys.

Second, they spoke a number of languages (vs. 6), although in

Jerusalem they probably used *koine* Greek and possibly some Aramaic. But the language factor is only part of the story. Luke names the various places of origin of those who were present. What is more, Luke constructs his description as a counterresponse to the table of nations in Genesis 10. Just as all humanity is included in the list of the nations surrounding Palestine at the time of the confusion of languages, so all humanity is represented by Luke's list in Acts 2. Every major nation surrounding Jerusalem in Luke's day is mentioned, and the people heard the disciples "speaking in the native language of each. Amazed and astonished, they asked. . . . 'How is it that we hear, each of us, in our own native language?'" (vss. 6b-8; see also vs. 11). Luke does not want us to miss this first picture of the universality of the gospel that is given for all nations.

Third, the list gives us more than an inclusive picture representing all the nations. It also gives us a hint of one of Luke's major agendas in Acts—the respect for and sensitivity to cultural and ethnic diversity within the unity of the church. These people are mentioned not only to have an inclusive list. They are included in order to highlight their unique importance and to bring attention to the fact that everyone in their OWN language was able to hear the gospel. Luke helps us see the tremendous variety represented by their various ethnic, linguistic, political, social, and historical backgrounds.

Fourth, Luke wants us to know that some of these people were "amazed," and that their curiosity and heightened interest motivated them to listen to Peter's upcoming explanation. At the same time, Luke notes that "others sneered" (vs. 13). We need to know that any time we begin listening carefully to the faith-searches of our neighbors, some will become interested in hearing what we have to say and others will not be open to hearing our witness.

Fifth, notice the order in which Luke tells the story. First, the disciples ENCOUNTER AND LISTEN to their neighbors. Only later will they speak to them. First, they are interested in who their neighbors are, where they come from, what languages they speak, and what their special and particular concerns and needs are. Only later will the disciples begin to speak through Peter.

REFLECTION

Luke's account calls us to examine our own "people blindness." We are all well aware of the tremendous influx of new immigrants into the United States during the last thirty-five years. Yet we seem to be developing a very selective vision which sees some people and is blind to others.

In other words, we are again faced with the question, "Who is my neighbor?" Please read Luke 10.25-37. We will not develop the entire parable here, but let's look at some relevant points. First, notice the question, and look carefully at Jesus' answer. The question asked by the "expert in the law" (vs. 25, NIV) is, "Who is my neighbor?" That is, who is the one I should love, as commanded in the law. Jesus tells the story, and in the end the one who loves his neighbor (or, in other words, the one who is neighborly) is the foreigner, the Samaritan, the one with whom the lawyer does not want to deal. In this story, the priest and the Levite are people-blind. They do not know how to love their neighbors as themselves. The foreign Samaritan does know how to love his neighbor, and in that act becomes the lawyer's neighbor as well. In other words, Jesus tells the story in such a way that the hated Samaritan ends up teaching the lawyer how to love his neighbor—and in that experience the lawyer begins to see the Samaritan as a neighbor to him.

Notice that the man who fell among thieves is not the principal character here. The principal issue is people-blindness. The central matter is being willing to love the other, being open to the other, being ready to listen to the other, being ready to "love my neighbor." We tend to have eyes but do not see. And here is one of the major barriers to effective evangelism. Chuck Kraft has emphasized the importance of this openness and sensitivity to our neighbor:

> The more we learn about the communication process, the more we become aware of just how crucial the receiver of the communication is to that process. . . . It. . . behooves us to learn as much as we can about what is going on at the [neighbor's] end when we attempt to communicate.[2]

We now know that there are a number of reasons why we become blind to other people. We know that those of us who live in urban areas will tend to restrict our meaningful relationships to a small group of trusted persons made up of family, a few friends, some church members, and a few business associates. We can drive the freeway and sail over thousands of persons whom we need not look at. We can drive into our places of business, park, go in to work, and leave for home at the end of the day, and never encounter anyone who lives in the area. We can commute to church and remain blind to those who live between our home and the church building. We know that urbanization—and especially a sense of the city being unsafe—will constantly push us to reduce the circle of our acquaintances.

Those of us who live in relatively rural settings also have forces which may produce people-blindness. We have long-standing associations with family, extended family, and friends. Our circle of acquaintances in rural areas tends to be larger than in urban areas. We know that newcomers to rural areas often find it very hard to break into the long-established webs of relationships which have been there for a long time. The long-term residents do not often make it a point to try to get to know the "newcomers." The new arrivals may remain new arrivals for years, with little meaningful contact with those who have lived in the area for a long time.

People-blindness is a major obstacle to our evangelization. Too often because we do not know, understand, or sensitively listen to our neighbor, we do not know what faith-questions our neighbor may be asking. Our lack of understanding, then, often leads us to give answers to questions that no one around us is asking.

At this stage we need to make a very important clarification. Relational evangelism is NOT essentially inviting someone to your church. Relational evangelism is sharing from your pilgrimage the ways in which you have experienced the presence of God, with the hope that this storytelling will open a channel for God to touch the life of your listener.

In North America there is another side to this. We know that there are many unchurched who have quite good reasons for NOT being in the church. In our conversations with them we need to listen carefully, non-defensively, and sensitively to the reasons why they are not in the church or may be very peripheral to the church. Often when we first begin to speak of faith issues with a neighbor, one of the first matters to arise is that person's past experiences and/or perceptions about the church. We need to listen carefully and take very seriously what is being said—while at the same time try to get beyond church in order to speak about the presence of God in our lives.

Let me illustrate the point. When my family and I moved to Holland, Michigan, my next-door neighbor came right over to explain the sprinkling system of my house. I will call him Al. Over the next several months we often talked when we were both working in the yard. I discovered that Al was downright fastidious about his lawn. It was immaculate: no dandelions, no dry spots, cut to a specified height, and beautifully groomed.

Well, one day I came out to work on the yard and Al was standing on his lawn with a sad look on his face, shaking his head. He had moles. The awful ridges where the moles had burrowed were clearly defacing Al's lawn. At this point we held our first "theological" conversation. Al turned to me and said, "Being a man of the cloth (he knew I was an ordained minister and former missionary), couldn't you do something about my moles?"

"Well, Al," I laughed, "I'm just not sure what the good Lord has in mind with those moles."

Al looked at me and chuckled. "I think I'm going to start talking to the man upstairs and see if he won't send these moles over to your yard." We laughed together and went about our work.

A few days later Al was standing in the same spot, shaking his head. "Now, Chuck," he said, "being a man of the cloth, can you explain this one to me? After I told you I was going to pray about these moles, they started heading in your direction, and I thought I had the problem solved. But look here."

Together Al and I studied the tunnels which the moles had dug.

"Just look at this!" he said. "They got to the edge of your property and turned right around and came back into mine! You must have something I don't have!"

Were we talking about moles? Or were we talking about someone who was obviously "faith-hungry" and very curious about my faith? Al clearly wanted to find out where I stood, and just as clearly I wanted to discover ways he and I might talk about our faith.

Months passed, and I slowly got to know Al. Then came the night when his wife (let's call her Ann) had a severe stroke. As soon as possible I went to their house to ask Al how she was doing. Ann was still in a coma. He did not know how long she would live.

After some time of speaking together, I asked Al if he would mind if I prayed. "Oh, I'd like that very much." So I talked to God with my arm around Al. I told God that we know our lives are in his hands, that we know he understands how we feel and suffer, that he knows how lonely and difficult this was for Al. I asked God to surround Ann with love and care, with his presence, and if it were his will, to bring her out of the coma to be able to speak again with Al.

Several days later, about midnight, there was a knock on our front door. It was Al. Could he come in? Al sat in our living room and told Jean and me that his wife had recently come out of the coma, was speaking again, and could recognize him. There was hope, he said, of some recovery. After a few minutes passed in conversation, Al got up to leave.

"Chuck," he said, "I came over to let you know about Ann. But I really came over to let you know about something else. I have not been able to sleep since the night Ann had her stroke. That is, up until two nights ago. Again, I could not sleep. Finally, I began weeping and talking to the man upstairs. I finally told him that my wife was his, that I was giving her over to him, and that I wanted to give my life to him for a second time—to come back to him, to believe in him again, and to begin to seek his presence—just as I had seen in your life. Chuck and Jean, it was about three o'clock in the morning, and I immediately fell asleep. I slept until almost five o'clock that afternoon. I slept like a baby.

"At five o'clock I got up, showered, and went to the hospital—and found that Ann had come out of her coma just that morning! I now know that the man upstairs really does care about us, and I am going to work on understanding him better and on getting closer to him. I just wanted you to know that."

As Al quickly stepped out of our front door and hurried back to his house, I was marveling at God's incredible grace. A conversation about moles in the lawn had initiated a process which was bringing

Al back to God!

But why should that have surprised me? Didn't Jesus always initiate conversations related to his hearer's own agendas? To the woman of Sychar he spoke of water (John 4). To the crowds that had been fed he spoke about bread (John 6). To Nicodemus he spoke about how to know God (John 3). To the rich young man he spoke about how to acquire salvation (Matt. 19). To blind Bartimaeus he talked about being able to see (Mark 10). The gospel is infinitely translatable. It always comes to the hearer in response to the hearer's questions, needs, and major concerns.

DISCUSSION

Now it's your turn. In the diagram below I have tried to illustrate the fact that all of us live in a number of different spheres or arenas. Each of these arenas represents a major web of relationships with people. Often there is little interaction between one arena and another. Often we ourselves are the only bridge between the various arenas of the social spheres of our context.

FIGURE 1: NATURAL ARENAS FOR RELATIONAL EVANGELISM

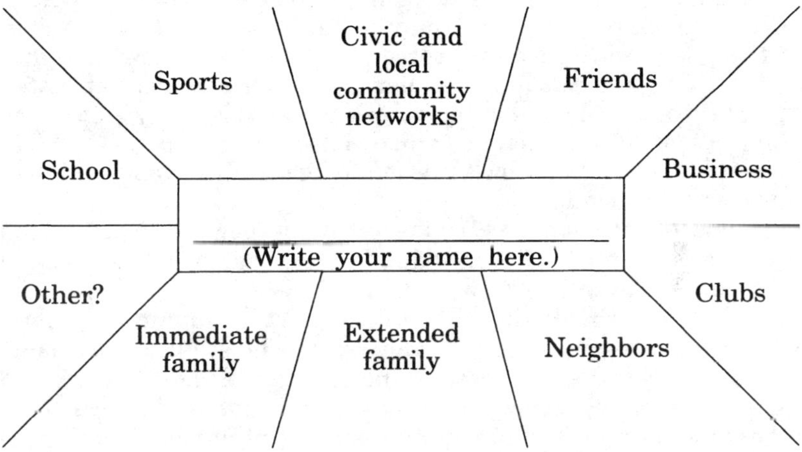

1. Let me suggest that each person in your evangelism group now take at least twenty minutes to reflect on those people with whom they come into contact over the period of a week. Following the diagram above, each person can consider those people that he or she knows in each of the arenas of life. (Feel free to add other arenas that are not depicted.) As participants remember who those persons are, they should write down their names in the various arenas of social activity. Include the names of bosses, business associates, employees, bowling partners, etc.

2. Now I want you to go a step further. In each arena circle the names of those persons who have at one time or another seemed to be "faith-hungry." Like Al, they on occasion have brought up something about church, about God, about faith, about your beliefs, etc. They seem interested in faith issues. They may or may not be church members.

3. It will be helpful to share with the group some stories about the individual you have thought of. Each member of your group may select one person to tell about.

You may want to subdivide the evangelism group into threes and fours and let them tell each other a story about someone they know in one of their webs of relationships, then share in what way they have begun to understand that this person may be "faith-hungry."

ACTION

Now comes the most crucial step of your journey in relational evangelism—and the most important part of your training for relational evangelism. Who is your neighbor?

A. Selection of a "neighbor"

Each member of your evangelism group needs to select a person out of all those they know who may be "faith-hungry." Each member of the group will select one person as their "neighbor." In other words, this is a careful and intentional selection of someone to listen to, care about, build a relationship with, and sensitively pilgrimage alongside at least as long as this evangelism group continues to meet. Let me suggest some steps for doing the above task, and then add some clarification.

1. The evangelism group may want to spend at least fifteen minutes in prayer together, asking God's guidance in the selection of the ones who will be their "neighbors."

2. The group should then maintain at least ten minutes of silence while members survey their webs of relationships and begin to listen to the Holy Spirit with regard to the selection of their "neighbors." For some, this selection will be easy, natural, and quick. It may take others the next week of prayer and soul-searching to select the one whom they will chose to love, listen to, and build a friendship with during the next ten weeks.

3. I suggest that the selection not be shared with the group at this time. That will happen later. Rather, three or four persons in the group may want to end this session by praying for the Holy Spirit's leading in this selection process.

4. It is very important at this point that each member of your evangelism group be called to commit themselves to fifteen minutes of additional prayer time per day—in addition to the fifteen minutes of prayer for the group, for their own faith pilgrimage, and for the evangelization of people in the community. Each member should

spend a minimum of fifteen minutes per day praying specifically for the "neighbor" whom he or she has selected. Tell God all you know about this person, ask God to bless this person, ask God to give you ears to hear what this person is saying about the deepest longings of his or her heart. Ask God to open natural, comfortable, spontaneous opportunities for you to build a meaningful relationship with this person, and for you to be able to witness about your faith-pilgrimage with this person.

B. Some clarifications

Several clarifications should be noted at this point:

1. The person whom you have chosen to be your "neighbor" is not to be depersonalized or degraded. He or she is not a thing, not an object, not a target, not a "pagan" or "heathen," not a "secular humanist," not a "soul going to hell." The person you have selected is first of all a PERSON. This person is loved so much by God that God gave his only Son for him or her. God wants so much to bring him or her into his sheepfold that he will leave the ninety-nine sheep in the corral and go out searching all night for the one lost sheep. Your selection of this person simply means that you have made a commitment and a choice to love and care. You are focusing your attention on this one person not in a manipulative or possessive way, but rather in a way that makes you available, open, sensitive, and ready to listen. This kind of prior commitment and openness on your part is just the opposite of depersonalization and manipulation.

2. If you have selected a faith-hungry person with whom you feel you can share faith, but who is of the opposite sex, please be careful. Faith-sharing can be a very intimate and deep matter, and issues of faith are closely associated with our sexuality. Be careful you do not confuse sexual attraction with a desire to be available to the faith-pilgrimage of your "neighbor."

3. Be prepared for the Holy Spirit to surprise you. Many people who have made a conscious choice to be available to someone have discovered that the Holy Spirit keeps bringing others, totally unexpected others, who are also faith-hungry. In fact, you may discover that the person you have selected will not allow you to share faith issues with him or her during the next ten weeks—and you may find that the Spirit will bring you someone else. Of course, that is O.K. What is most important is that you be open and available to the faith issues of your "neighbor," whoever the Spirit brings before you.

4. Remember that what you will seek to share with your neighbor is not so much yourself, nor your church, nor "religion" in general. Rather, you will seek to share Jesus. You hope to be able to "witness," to testify about those instances in your pilgrimage when you were absolutely sure that God was there through faith in Jesus Christ, by the working of the Holy Spirit.

[1] Corwin Smidt and James Penning, "Priorities for the Church: What RCA Clergy Think are the Key Tasks of the Local Church in the Nineties," The *Church Herald* (XLVII:8, August 1990), pp. 20-23.

[2] Charles Kraft, *Communication Theory for Christian Witness*, (Nashville: Abingdon, 1983), p. 89.

CHAPTER FOUR

Listening to Your Neighbor

(Acts 2.14-15)

Once we have begun to notice, listen to, and make ourselves available for our neighbor, we can begin to understand our neighbor more completely. Notice that relational evangelism does not begin with speaking—it begins with LISTENING. And it may take a very significant amount of time and attention to listen well before we have won the right to speak.

EXPOSITION

Please read Acts 2.14-15. Luke's narrative in Acts emphasizes Peter's ability to listen. He clearly heard what the people in the street were saying—that the disciples must be drunk. Peter begins his conversation by addressing both the visiting devout ones and the residents of Jerusalem. He begins by speaking precisely to the issue that is uppermost in the minds of his hearers. "They are filled with new wine" (vs. 13). Peter does not dispute their opinion that the disciples are behaving strangely. Rather, he offers another explanation for their unorthodox behavior: that rather than reeling from the effects of alcohol ("It is only nine o'clock in the morning"), the disciples are giddy from the effects of being impacted by the Holy Spirit whose coming was foretold by the prophet Joel (vss. 15-16). Peter knows his hearers, understands them, and presents his case along particular lines that are compatible with their particular way of viewing things. Peter listens well.

Peter's behavior serves as a model and stimulus for us. Last week you were asked to select one person as your "neighbor," on whom you will focus your attention and to whom you will begin to listen sensitively and intentionally. Now you need to ask some deeply insightful questions regarding your selective hearing. All of us hear selectively. We hear some things and block out others. When it comes to listening to our neighbor we need to be very careful and sensitive to the way we listen. We will be helped in our listening if we understand some things about communication theory.

In our evangelistic efforts we often forget that our most effective bridges with our unchurched neighbors involves our human existence—day-to-day problems, personal frailties, and intimate experiences. We can draw from our own spiritual journeys to the degree that we have experienced God's presence in those ordinary, day-to-day matters of human life.

Our neighbor's life involves many experiences that are like our own, experiences which also need to be illuminated by the grace of Jesus Christ. Matters related to possessions, finances, ambitions, fears, children, sex, marriage, death, physical fitness, jobs, schools—all of these are subjects which can trigger an appropriate word, an act of love and concern, a sharing of the grace of God with your neighbor. Matters of faith cannot be divorced from our ordinary, everyday lives. Faith must be relevant. What keeps your witness from being proselytism (which seeks only to win another adherent to your church) is precisely your witness to God's abounding grace in the day-to-day events of human existence. Again, you see why the matter of understanding our own faith pilgrimage is so vital for relational evangelism. You will share nothing if you have nothing to share.

Picture yourself approaching and beginning to acquaint yourself with your neighbor. You will listen carefully to your neighbor if you remember that your neighbor is a whole person. Not only is your neighbor a unified composite of the physical, emotional, mental, and spiritual—this person is also the product of a significant number of relationships and experiences. All of these go together to create an amazingly unique individual, different from you and different from anyone else you know.

Within that wholeness, your neighbor has various dimensions, and it is important that you know something about them. The following diagram illustrates the various aspects of who your neighbor is, as seen from the point of view of communication theory. Let's begin with the central core issues of your neighbor's identity, and work outward.

FIGURE 2: DIMENSIONS OF YOUR NEIGHBOR'S IDENTITY

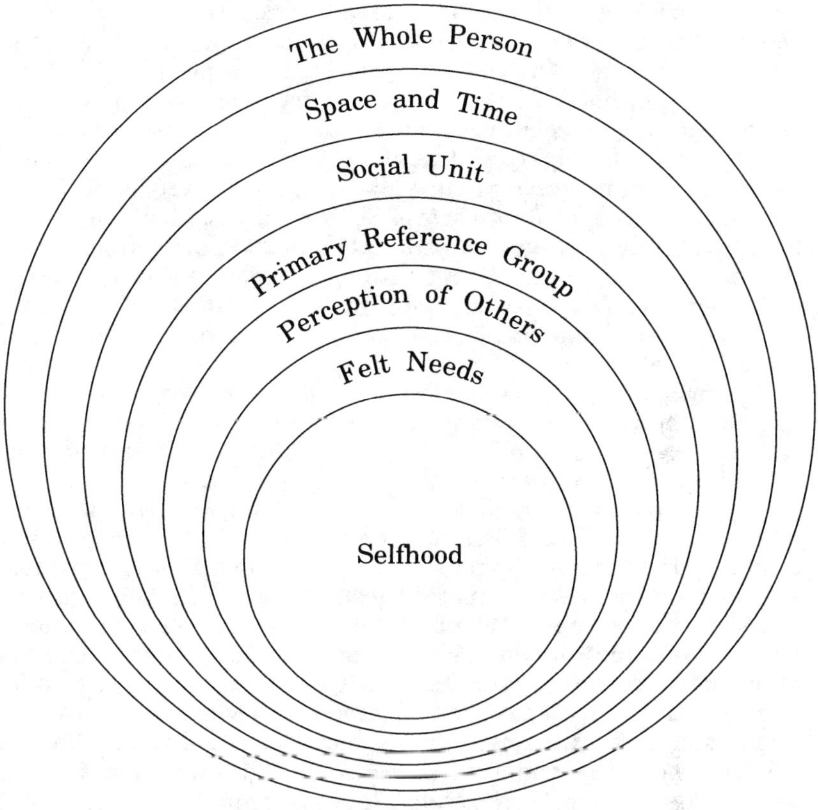

First, your neighbor holds a certain self-concept. That may be a very positive one, full of self-assertion, self-confidence, and power. Or it may be a negative one, full of guilt, inferiority, and self-doubt. Clearly the way you go about witnessing to your neighbor will be influenced by how you understand your neighbor's self-concept. At a very deep level, the gospel comes to transform all of us to become able to forgive ourselves, accept ourselves, and love ourselves.

Second, your neighbor has both surface and deep-level felt needs to which your friendship, your witness, and the gospel itself may be addressed. More than any other level, this arena is the one at which the gospel may impact your neighbor. In his ministry, Jesus always responded directly to the particular felt needs of his hearers. We are called upon to do the same. Have you listened carefully enough to your neighbor to be able to describe your neighbor's deep-seated felt needs?

Third, your neighbor has certain perceptions of others, including you. Your neighbor may like people or hate people. Your neighbor may be narrowly judgmental or broadly accepting. Clearly what your neighbor thinks of others will color the way you witness, the stories you tell, and the way you present the gospel.

Fourth, your neighbor is part of a primary reference group. There are certain people whom your neighbor considers most significant. These may be family, close friends, or intimate associates whose friendship your neighbor highly values. You will often discover who these people are by listening carefully to your neighbor's conversation. Invariably your neighbor will talk about what is happening in the lives of these people. What is being signaled in the conversation is not only WHAT may be happening, but how your neighbor perceives his or her ongoing relationship with these very important people.

This primary reference group may or may not have some Christians in it. It may be a strongly anti-Christian group. Your neighbor will hear your words and filter them according to how they interface with issues related to this primary reference group.

Zacchaeus (Luke 19) and Nicodemus (John 3) were two very different types of individuals. Yet they had something very much in common. They were conscious of their reference groups, and they soon came to realize the impact of Jesus' message on their relationship with these groups. When Zacchaeus the tax collector came to experience a radical conversion in his encounter with Jesus, he immediately recognized that he must correct the inequities that he had perpetrated in the taxation system, return what was unlawfully taken, and make restitution for the harm caused. I'm sure he was well aware of the personal and professional cost this course of action would take. Nicodemus the rabbi, on the other hand, wanted to avoid conflict with his primary group, so he went to Jesus by night. But very soon he discovered that an acceptance of Jesus' message would mean radical rethinking of many ideas held dear by his colleagues. John leads us to believe that quite a process was involved as Nicodemus was converted away from his primary reference group and to Jesus Christ (see John 7.50-52; 19.38-42).

Fifth, your neighbor belongs to a certain larger social unit which strongly impacts the way your neighbor will filter your witness. If your witness directly conflicts with values held by the larger social unit which is important to your neighbor, your message will not be heard.

For example, it may be that you have selected a teenager as your special neighbor during these weeks. Whatever you offer by way of witness will be filtered by that teenager's relationships with other teenagers. Your witness may entail too high a price if it challenges his or her relationships with other teenagers. In many parts of the world, acceptance of the gospel will mean ostracism from one's most important social arenas, and perhaps social and physical suffering as well. As North America becomes less and less a "Christian" nation, we need to be prepared to deal with the social price which some of our neighbors may have to pay when they accept Jesus Christ and become responsible members of the church.

Finally, there is the matter of space and time. Often our witness of the gospel is dependent on timing and is influenced by where it takes place. You remember the story of Al in Chapter Three? It took over two years, and it took a particular crisis moment before I had the opportunity to pray with Al. It also took intentionality and caring on my part to go over to speak with him. It was the right time, and his home was at that point the right place. Even so, it took even more time until he was ready to be encountered by God—in his case while he was alone, unable to sleep.

In seeking opportunities to witness to our faith through relational evangelism, we need to be very sensitive to the work of the Holy Spirit in giving us the right time and the right place—and then we need to be ready and willing to witness when the Spirit presents us with that opportunity. For example, Philip had to sit by the side of a dusty road and wait for the Ethiopian to go by (Acts 8.26-39).

Relational evangelism is as simple as being interested in someone and wanting to comfort him or her with the comfort you have received from God. Yet it is as complicated as all the various arenas we have been looking at in answer to the question, "Who is my neighbor?" You may be saying at this point, "But I don't know all of this about my neighbor—and, moreover, I don't want to pry or be nosy." Exactly. Our study of the various arenas of your neighbor's makeup has two purposes.

First, it will in fact show you all the many things you DO NOT know about your neighbor. Too often we want to evangelize people while knowing little about them! Too often we are more interested in being done with the task of evangelizing than we are in getting to know the evangelized. You cannot share your own faith pilgrimage until you are willing to get to know who your neighbor is—not in a nosy sort of way, but in a way that says, "I care about you, I'm interested in you, and I want to get to know you."

Second, a deeper understanding of the various arenas of your neighbor's life will help you listen more carefully. The next time you talk together, try to hear things which may begin to fill in some of the blanks. You will discover that your neighbor has been telling you a lot more than you have been hearing.

REFLECTION

I got on an airplane in Pittsburgh. I had an aisle seat toward the front, where I like it. As is my custom, I sat back, relaxed, closed my eyes, and prepared to fall asleep as soon as the tires left the ground. Then the flight attendant tapped me on the shoulder.

"Sir, you look so relaxed and like you enjoy plane travel so much, could I ask a favor of you? You see the woman across the aisle and up one row? She is terribly afraid of flying and is nearly hysterical, but she must get to Grand Rapids today. Would you be willing to sit beside her?"

Well, I really wanted to sleep. In fact, I was half asleep already. But who could refuse a request like that? "Who, if your child asks for bread, will give a stone?" (Matt. 7.9). I nodded to the flight attendant and moved over to the other side of the airplane.

Her name could have been Jane. She was fidgeting and biting her nails. Her eyes were slits, she held her shoulders too high, and her heals dug into the bottom of the seat.

Well, Jane and I ended up talking non-stop for the next ninety minutes. When we landed in Grand Rapids she was very surprised. She told me that she had never enjoyed a plane ride before in her life, but this one had been fun, and she hadn't even noticed the time go by. Why? Because I began asking her questions about herself, being genuinely interested in her—and I slowly began to understand who she was.

Jane was going back to Muskegon, where she and her husband had been living for three years. They had no friends, did not know anyone, and it looked like her husband was going to lose the job for which he had moved there in the first place. Jane and her husband were originally from Pittsburgh. He had been Roman Catholic, and she Methodist. They had been married twenty years ago, and had dropped out of the church altogether. His family did not accept her, and her family did not accept him.

Then Jane told me the real reason why she was afraid of flying. She was going back to a city where she had no friends, no church, and possibly no income for their family of six. As if that were not enough, she had just been diagnosed by her doctor in Pittsburgh as being in the beginning stages of multiple sclerosis. She wasn't afraid of flying; she was afraid of dying.

Why had she let me into her life so deeply and so quickly? Well, sometimes it is safer to talk to strangers than to those close to us. But I believe there was another reason. Somewhere in the early stages of the conversation, before she told me about her health problems, I told her about when I almost died from typhoid fever. I told her about the terrible depression, about the hallucinations at night and the exhaustion by day. I told her about the three women who came to pray with me and to sit with me for at least an hour. I told her about how during their prayers one of the women had said, "Let Chuck see your light in his darkness of despair." I had felt like I was at the bottom of a deep, deep well and could hardly see the light at the top.

But when that sister prayed, suddenly there was a flash of bright, white, warm enveloping light—not up at the top of the well, but down in the very bottom, just where I was. And I told Jane that I had felt the light lift me, pull me, draw me up out of that despair and fear—toward hope and a desire for new life. I told her that it still took some time for me to come back to health, but the steps toward wholeness began with that moment.

It was at that stage that she began to weep and tell me of her visit just that morning to her doctor in Pittsburgh.

We spent the last fifteen minutes of that flight praying and crying together. She placed her life, that of her husband and family, their future, and her deepest fears in the hands of God. Together we told Jesus that we believed that he loved her and her family. I told her that I had no answers that would explain why we sometimes get into such difficult situations. But I told her that God's presence is a sustaining presence as we open ourselves to him, and especially as we allow others to minister to us.

Later when I got home I called a friend of mine who was a pastor of a large church in her city. It turned out that my friend's church building was only a few blocks away from where Jane lived. I never found out how Jane fared, but on that airplane I learned again that compassionate listening opens the avenue for sensitive witness.

Now it is your turn. Imagine in your mind's eye the face of your neighbor. Hold in your mind a picture of who that person is—his or her values, priorities, dreams, felt needs, recent joys, anxieties, difficulties, and triumphs. You may or may not know your neighbor very well, but if you review those things you have already heard from your neighbor, you may discover that you know more than you thought. Now take a blank sheet of paper and write a one-page description of your neighbor, as if you were introducing her or him to someone in your group. Write down everything you think you know about your neighbor. Also include questions concerning matters which you now realize you don't know.

DISCUSSION

At this point I suggest subdividing the group to form groups of two or three. Each member of a small group should then take no more than ten minutes to introduce his or her neighbor to the others in the group. The others should listen carefully and possibly ask some questions about matters they may not fully understand. The presenters may wish to reflect on their perceptions of their neighbors in terms of their neighbors' spiritual journeys. Finally, the presenters may want to suggest what they consider to be appropriate actions, attitudes, responses, or questions to be addressed to their neighbors in the future. What are some intentional ways whereby you may listen more carefully to your neighbor's pilgrimage? What specific actions might you take to deepen your friendship with your neighbor in a natural, caring, and unforced manner? Remember that all aspects of human life (physical, emotional, psychological, spiritual, vocational, relational, social, educational, political, economic, etc.) are relevant at this point.

ACTION

This gathering of your evangelism group has not concluded until you have spent some significant time in prayer. I suggest that the members remain in their smaller groups of twos and threes. They should spend at least fifteen minutes praying for each other and especially for the neighbors of whom each has spoken. Remember that earlier you committed yourself to pray for fifteen minutes each day for the others in your group. Now commit yourself during this coming week to pray not only for the members of your group, but also for the neighbors about whom you heard in your small group.

CHAPTER FIVE

Communicating the Gospel with Your Neighbor

(Acts 2.16-36)

Effective communication does not depend ultimately on the communicator; it depends on the hearer. The one who communicates the message needs to be clear, directed, and intentional about the way the message is presented. But in the final analysis it is the listener who will or will not give permission for the message to really be heard.

Jesus referred to this truth of communication when he explained why he spoke in parables. Using the words of Deuteronomy 29, Jeremiah 5, Ezekiel 12, and Isaiah 6, Jesus spoke of those who "will indeed listen, but never understand . . . indeed look, but never perceive" (Matt. 13.14). Jesus mentioned this in relation to the parable of the soils. Clearly, the same sower sowed the same seed everywhere. But the hearers differed in their response to the gospel. In some cases the communication of the gospel produced fruit, but in others it did not. The wonder of communication involves a miracle of hearing. The listener determines the appropriateness, the meaning, the value, and the cost of what the communicator is wanting to convey. Both inside and outside the church we need to be acutely aware of the hearer's role in communication.

I was struck by this one day in the case of a vibrant, energetic, happy, creative woman we will call Sally. Sally was part of a study group in a course on prayer at the seminary where I was teaching.

I had been asked to be the facilitator of this small group that would meet for two hours every Thursday afternoon. Each week the members of the group were to read a section of the workbook we were using and to follow the suggestions made there.

One Thursday I had over-programmed myself and was running late. I came hurrying in for our group meeting. Breathless, I sat down, looked around the group, and asked the question I had given them each previous week. "Well, what did you learn this week?" I was totally unprepared for the response.

I had barely gotten the question out when Sally began to weep uncontrollably. I was taken completely by surprise. I looked around the group, and they also seemed at a loss. As the weeping turned to sobs, I asked Sally if she was willing to share her story with us. Nodding, she began.

"All my life I have been in the church, hearing sermons, listening to Sunday school lessons, learning the Bible. I came here to seminary to prepare for ministry in the church, and I have studied and learned even more. But there is something basic that I had never learned until late last night.

"I always knew that God is love, and that Jesus loves everyone. I took that for granted. But last night, while I was following the prayer exercises for this group, I came to realize something I had never really known before. I had done the assigned reading and had begun to talk to Jesus about it when suddenly an overwhelming presence seemed to surround me. There was someone standing beside me. I opened my eyes and looked up, expecting to see someone. Instead, I heard a voice as clearly as if it had spoken out loud.

'Sally I love *YOU*.'

"And then I knew something I had never really known before: Jesus loves ME!"

Sally's tears had by now turned into a great big grin of deep rejoicing. It was so thoroughly joyful that I discovered all the rest of us in the group were smiling back at her!

"He loves ME! I know it because he told me. I know it because I felt it in a way I had never sensed before. I know it because something inside me has drastically changed. I am different today. Jesus loves ME!"

Two years later I had a chance to have dinner with Sally and a group of other students from her graduating class. Surrounded by a number of people, with everyone creating quite a lot of confusion with their various conversations, Sally leaned across the table and grinned at me with that same deep smile of pure joy I remembered from before.

"Chuck, you remember that discussion group on prayer that you led? You remember when I burst out crying one afternoon? I haven't been the same since. I find that my self-esteem and self-image, my relationship to my husband and my children, my ministry in my church, my Bible study and seminary education—all have changed. I have a sense of the presence of Jesus in my life like never before. I have been able to minister to others and see their lives transformed in ways I never imagined. My sense of direction and call are wonderfully clear and powerfully motivating. I am a different person. I just thought you would like to know."

And then it was my turn to cry.

EXPOSITION

If communication depends not so much on the communicator, but on the one who receives the communication, then it is of utmost importance that we learn to present our message in a way that makes sense to our hearers. Sally had always heard, but had never really heard the most basic truth of the gospel—that Jesus loved her. It was in the midst of a particular set of circumstances that she was enabled to finally hear and understand. Through the reading, exercises in prayer, and small group discussion, the message had finally been communicated in a way that was understandable for Sally.

Peter's message in Acts 2 is a particularly significant illustration of this careful crafting of the communication for the sake of the hearers. Please read Acts 2.16-36.

Whether or not Luke gives us Peter's entire speech here is not really an issue. What is important is to look at Peter's sermon from the perspective of the hearers. And when we take the hearers into account, we see that the address is masterfully crafted to match who they are, their point of view, their concerns, their questions. Briefly, let me point out some of the major points of Peter's sermon to show you how well they match the agendas of Peter's hearers.

First, Peter begins by explaining the disciples' strange behavior. He says that the disciples are giddy with the presence of the Holy Spirit, whose coming had been foretold long ago in Old Testament passages that were common fare for the hearers. Numbers 11, Isaiah 44, Ezekiel 39, Psalm 105 and Joel 2 were well-known passages that struck familiar chords of Messianic expectation and future hope in the hearts of those present. And the behavior of the disciples matched that which was foretold. The fulfillment of prophecy, the coming of that which had been promised, had always been understood in Israel as a sign of God's work and of the authenticity of the vessel through whom God chose to work. Given Israelite history and world view, quoting these texts was a splendid way to get their attention.

Second, the hearers had been around Jerusalem for some time and had heard of the events surrounding the crucifixion of Jesus of Nazareth. They apparently knew that he had been a wonder worker, and the rumors about him had not yet died down.

Third, basing himself again on the familiar words of Psalm 16, Peter speaks about his own experience. Beginning with an interpretation of the Psalm that would leave open the possibility that David was speaking of another who would rise from the dead, Peter tells his hearers about his own faith pilgrimage, about what he and the others had witnessed. "This Jesus God raised up, and of that all of us are witnesses" (vs. 32).

Fourth, Peter affirms the ascension of Jesus, the result of which is the sending of the Holy Spirit. Again, Peter returns to the matter of explaining the strange behavior of these who had burst into the street from that room, whose speech everyone had heard in their own language. This has happened, says Peter, because the ascended Jesus "has poured out [the Holy Spirit] that you both see and hear" (vs. 33).

"Therefore, let the entire house of Israel know with certainty that God has made him both Lord and Messiah, this Jesus whom you crucified" (vs. 36).

Peter does four things at once in his address. First, he carefully crafts his message to respond to the immediate question of the hearers: how to explain the strange behavior of these people whom they hear speaking in their native languages. Second, he draws his supporting arguments from a source which his hearers hold as authoritative: the Old Testament. Third, he works in his own personal experience and witnesses to what he and the others have seen. Fourth, Peter declares the basic message of the gospel: that Jesus is the Christ.

REFLECTION

Peter's Pentecost address serves as a model for us. But it helps us only if we allow it to stimulate our own reflection on the way we may present the gospel message to our neighbors. In the first place, I want you to notice that Peter combines both his subjective experience and his objective understanding of truth. Jesus is the Christ not only because Peter saw the resurrection, but because the resurrection is a fulfillment of the prophecies. At the same time, the disciples are acting strangely because they have EXPERIENCED the fulfillment of those promises. In communicating the gospel, both propositional truth and existential experience need to be interwoven together like the warp and woof of a piece of cloth. Experience without truth is meaningless. Logical propositions without life-changing experiences are irrelevant.

The way we present our message has to do with bridging the emotional, spiritual, physical, and cultural distance between ourselves and our neighbor. This cultural distance involves the measure of difference that may exist between the way you perceive your world and the way your neighbor sees his or her world. And here we need to be aware of an axiom of effective gospel communication:

THE GREATER THE PERSONAL AND/OR CULTURAL DISTANCE BETWEEN OURSELVES AND OUR NEIGHBOR, THE MORE INTENTIONAL AND PRECISE WE MUST BE IN PRESENTING THE GOSPEL MESSAGE.

In Acts 1.8 Jesus tells the disciples that they will be witnesses "in Jerusalem, in all Judea and Samaria, and to the ends of the earth." Although these are geographic terms, they mean much more than that. Essentially, Jesus was referring to the personal and cultural distance between the disciples and the hearers of the message. Luke, in fact, uses this as the basic outline of the book of Acts to demonstrate the increasing cultural and personal expansion of the gospel that is intended for all the peoples of the world.

This has tremendous implications for us. Think now of the person you have chosen as your neighbor for this study. Think about the *differences* between you and your neighbor. Maybe a diagram will help. In Figure 3 below notice that the greater the personal and cultural distance, the higher will be the barrier to effectively communicate with your neighbor. Those barriers consist of differences in perspective with regard to personal life, emotions, faith, social class, deep values, language, and world view. The greater the differences between you and your neighbor, the more intentional and careful you need to be in your communication, so that the meaning which your neighbor ascribes to what you are saying is in fact what you intended to say.

FIGURE 3: BARRIERS TO GOSPEL COMMUNICATION

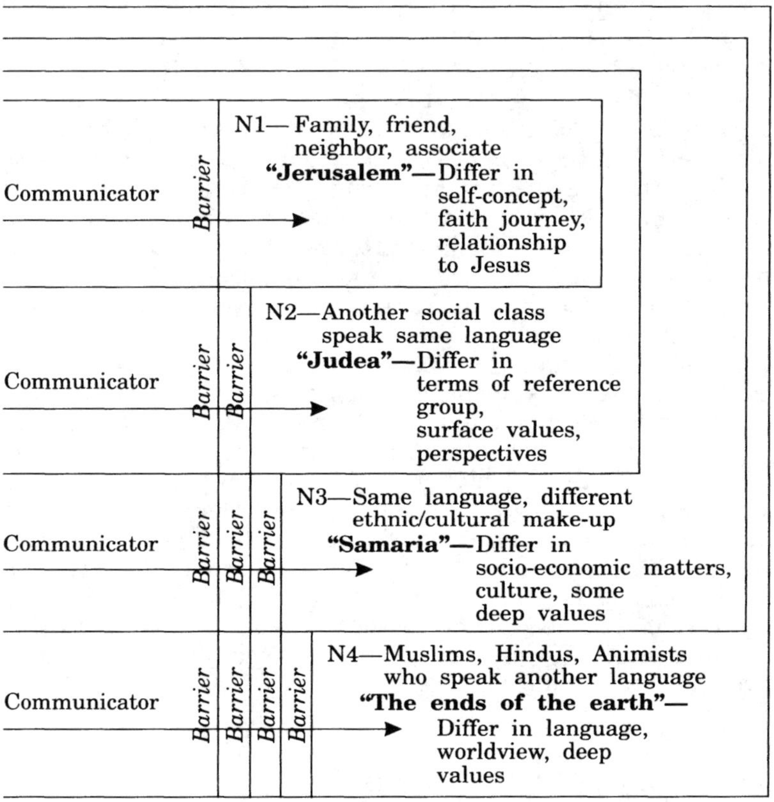

So the secret of witnessing to your neighbor is to understand as completely as possible the way your neighbor views reality and what your neighbor considers important. Then strive to be authentically yourself, drawing from your pilgrimage but presenting your witness in a way that will be meaningful for your neighbor. As Robert Bast said, "Understanding people is the necessary first step in being able to minister to them. Knowing what makes members of (the baby boom generation) tick will come only with a willingness to listen to their needs."[1]

Jesus did this constantly in his ministry. Your group might want to study one of the following examples, looking at the way Jesus crafted his message in ways that were uniquely suited to each hearer.

a. Jesus and Nathaniel (John 1)
b. Jesus and Simon Peter (Luke 5.1-11)

c. Jesus and the Samaritan woman of Sychar (John 4)
d. Jesus and Martha (John 11.25-26)
e. Jesus and the paralytic (Luke 5)
f. Jesus and the rich young man (Matt. 19)
g. Jesus and the woman caught in adultery (John 8)
h. Jesus and Zacchaeus (Luke 19)
i. Jesus and the hungry crowd (John 6)

Later Philip would follow this process when he met the Ethiopian on the road and discovered that the Ethiopian was reading from Isaiah and was seeking someone to explain it to him (Acts 8). Peter would do the same when he met with Cornelius (Acts 10). And Paul would develop the process even more when he encountered the philosophers of Athens (Acts 17). In fact, Paul later articulated this as a personalized principle of the church's mission: "I have become all things to all people, so that I might by all means save some" (1 Cor. 9.22). Our heart's desire in all of this is for our hearers to experience what Sally did, the overwhelming sensation of being wrapped in the arms of a loving God.

You may be asking how to do this. The first step in learning how to sensitively develop your message is to become aware of WHAT YOU DO NOT KNOW. You may discover that you really do not know your neighbor well enough to be able to effectively present your witness. Then you need to go back to Chapter Four and think through some of those issues again as you seek ways to deepen your relationship with your neighbor. Or you may discover that you know your neighbor quite well, but you do not know the basics of the gospel. Maybe you have not experienced deeply enough the gospel's impact in your own faith pilgrimage and so you are not able to retell your experience in a way that is meaningful to your neighbor. In that case, you may want to go back to Chapter Two and reflect longer on the times, places, and ways in which you discovered God's loving presence in your life.

The second step is to take some time to reflect on the differences between you and your neighbor. It is important that you learn to view reality through the eyes of your neighbor. We tend to project on others the way we see things. That often causes deep misunderstandings. As you have developed a friendship with your neighbor, can you articulate the way your neighbor looks at the world? Whether you agree with them or not, can you express your neighbor's deepest values and most urgent felt needs?

The third step is to begin to consider what parts of your own spiritual pilgrimage might be helpful for your neighbor. At this stage you have no idea whether you will ever get a chance to say these things to your neighbor. But if you had a chance to tell your story to your neighbor, how would you do that? Which of your own experiences, coupled with truths of Scripture regarding Jesus Christ, would you want to briefly express?

The fourth step is to pray. In Chapter Seven we will look more carefully at the role of the Holy Spirit in the process of relational evangelism. However, you need to take it into consideration at this point as well. Peter encourages all Christians to "always be prepared to give an answer to everyone who asks you to give the reason for the hope that you have" (1 Pet. 3:15, NIV). But the appropriate presentation of our witness for our neighbor is not our task alone. It also involves the Holy Spirit's revelation to us. When Jesus sent out the twelve on their first mission (Matt. 10), he promised that through the Holy Spirit he would give them the appropriate words. When we as his disciples are called upon to witness, Jesus promises that "what you are to say will be given to you at that time, for it is not you who speak, but the Spirit of your Father speaking through you" (Matt. 10.19-20; see also Luke 21 and Mark 13).

The fifth step is to be aware of the Lord's timing. We are to be prepared to give an answer to our neighbor. But when and how that opportunity will arise is a matter which only the Holy Spirit knows. In fact, the way our witness to our neighbor actually happens will probably surprise us in its unexpected form and timing. If we are not prepared, it may not happen at all. But on the other hand, if we try to force it because we have now "prepared our speech," so to speak, and are only looking for a time to dump the whole load on our neighbor, we may miss a chance to witness effectively, lovingly, sensitively, and appropriately. The time is really our neighbor's choice, and happens by the work of the Holy Spirit. We are to anticipate hopefully, patiently, and prayerfully the moment when such a time may naturally arise—and be prepared to let the Holy Spirit give us the right words.

One of my evangelism class students (let's call her Nancy) mentioned how this factor had surprised her. Nancy had chosen as a neighbor a girl that made a living through prostitution in a nearby town. She had befriended the girl and had spent quite a bit of time and energy getting to know her. Weeks had gone by and she had not yet had the chance to witness with regard to any faith issues. She was getting frustrated and impatient, but she continued to prepare and to pray.

Well, it so happened that a group of her friends were going to Detroit to watch a baseball game. Nancy "happened" to run into the girl one day and casually mentioned that she was going to Detroit to the game. The girl's eyes lit up. Could she come along? Nancy told my evangelism class that she felt terribly awkward at this point. The women she was going to Detroit with were the prim and proper types, quite different from this girl. What would they think about bringing her along? Nancy said that in that instant it was as though she heard a voice speaking in her head: "Take her along."

"Sure, we'd love to have you," she heard herself say. "I'm driving the van, so you can sit next to me, up front."

I remember the tears running down Nancy's cheeks as she told us of that drive to Detroit. They had barely gotten on the freeway when the girl asked Nancy, "Do you believe there is a God?"

Nancy was able to respond by telling of an experience when she was absolutely sure that God was there. Nancy was prepared, because for weeks she had been thinking and praying about this moment. "But," Nancy told us, "the amazing thing was that the story I told the girl was one I had not thought of in years. And the words—the way I said them and the emotions involved in them—were something beyond anything I had prepared for." The girl listened intently, tears beginning to flow.

"But what surprised me even more," Nancy told us, "was that the girl responded with another question. To my surprise, in response to the girl's second question, a woman in the second seat of the van began telling a story of a time when she was deeply impacted by the presence of God. Then another woman told her story. Then another. We ended up singing. The girl, my neighbor, sat quietly weeping beside me, profoundly moved."

Nancy finished the story for the evangelism class in a quiet voice of marvel and wonder. "When we arrived at the stadium parking lot and began to get out of the van, the girl asked us if we would put our arms around her and pray with her. She wanted to commit her life to Jesus. Seldom have I felt the presence of God as I felt it that afternoon standing in that parking lot," Nancy told us, "these women and I with our arms around my neighbor, listening to her tell Jesus that she wanted to follow him."

DISCUSSION

This week when your evangelism group gathers, I suggest that the first fifteen minutes be spent reporting to each other what you have been experiencing lately in developing your friendship with the person you chose as your neighbor.

Then spend the next ten minutes praying for each other and for the neighbors that have been mentioned, giving thanks and offering petitions as appropriate.

Now the group should be prepared for further reflection and discussion. Ask each member to spend fifteen minutes writing a one-page presentation of the good news as they would like to share it with the person they have chosen as their neighbor. Ask them to write this as a specially personalized message, suited just for their neighbor.

Here are a few suggestions you might want to consider:

1. Avoid church jargon and "God-talk."

2. Strive to communicate within the conceptual framework of your neighbor.

3. Incorporate something out of your own pilgrimage that is an appropriate illustration of the ideas you want to convey.

4. Frame the message in a way that feels natural and sensitive, within the bounds of the type of friendship you have been developing with your neighbor.

5. Give some thought to whether there may be some things you need to be DOING with regard to your neighbor—things that might communicate as well or better than words.

6. Remember that the Holy Spirit may have some surprises in store. You may never get a chance to share what you have prepared. But it will help you get ready to witness authentically and sensitively when the Spirit offers you the opportunity. When that time comes, you can forget about what you have written and just speak from your heart, knowing that the Spirit will give you the appropriate words.

7. Finally, no matter how you craft your communication, remember that our message is always the same. Ultimately, we do not speak about ourselves; *we speak of Jesus the Christ* (Acts 2.22-36).

Now I suggest regrouping in twos and threes. (These may or may not be the same small groups as before.) Take about twenty minutes and have the members of the group read their messages to the others in their small group. The small groups should end their time together by spending ten minutes or so in prayer for each other and for their neighbors.

ACTION

I suggest the following action steps for the coming week:

1. Continue the discipline of fifteen minutes of daily prayer for the members of your evangelism group, along with fifteen minutes of daily prayer for your neighbor.

2. Begin to think of, jot down, and carry out specific action steps that may respond in appropriate ways to your neighbor's felt needs. Think of ways to show that you care about your neighbor as a person, that you care even more deeply now that you have begun to know some of your neighbor's pilgrimage in the context of your friendship. (By the way, you may discover that many of these ideas as to what you can do with and for your neighbor may come to you during your prayer time. Take them as from the Lord. Jot them down right then—and commit yourself to finding time and ways to DO them.)

[1] Robert Bast, "Where a Generation Hungers," the *Church Herald* (XLVIII:4, April 1991), p. 11. This is one of the outstanding articles in this issue of the *Church Herald* that discuss the unique opportunities and challenges involved in evangelizing the baby boom

generation. See also Robert Bast, *The Missing Generation: The Church's Ministry with the Baby Boom Generation* (Grand Rapids: Reformed Church Press, 1991).

CHAPTER SIX

Clarifying Your Motivations and Goals in Evangelism

(Acts 2.37)

Sunrise was at 5:35 that morning. My family and I had arrived late the night before and had hoped to be able to sleep in a little. But life in Tuxtla Gutierrez, the capital of the state of Chiapas, Mexico, begins early. The vendors were just beginning to walk by our open windows shouting out their wares, "tortillas, pan, naranjas," when we heard the high-pitched whine of a small airplane overhead. Suddenly a booming voice came from the loudspeakers tied to the underside of its wings. God's judgement was near. It was imperative that we repent and accept Jesus Christ as our Savior.

My wife and I rushed to the window just in time to see the man in the open door of the airplane dump out hundreds of leaflets. As they floated down to us, we were told by the loudspeaker that this had been a message, courtesy of the Gospel from the Air Mission. We had just been evangelized. The rest of the day we joined our neighbors trying to clean up the mess that those hundreds of pamphlets had made in our streets and yards.

Although this true story is clearly a caricature of evangelism, it serves to emphasize one of our greatest difficulties in this area. Too often our evangelistic efforts are not effective because our long-range objectives have not been carefully examined. Too often we simply don't know what evangelism is. And clarification is not easy, partly because of our own uncertainties about the ultimate goals of our evangelistic efforts, and partly because we are unclear as to our motivations for being involved in it in the first place. In this chapter we want to examine these two areas: What motivates you to want to evangelize your neighbor? And how will you know when you have accomplished your evangelistic task? But first, let's go back to Peter's first sermon in Acts 2.

EXPOSITION

Please read Acts 2.37. Those who heard Peter's sermon and took it to heart were moved by the Holy Spirit to ask the foundational question with which this chapter deals: "What shall we do?"

Peter's hearers were making certain judgments concerning the motivation and authenticity of the disciples. And they were weighing the implications of what they had just heard, anxious to know what would be an appropriate response to Peter's message. "What shall we do? What do you expect from us?"

There will come a time when your neighbor will be asking a similar question. And it is one which you need to be prepared to answer. Your preparation is important not just because you must have the right answer for your neighbor. Rather, it is important that you reflect on this question *for the sake of your own integrity*. One of the primary ways we can keep relational evangelism from becoming manipulative and coercive is to be absolutely clear within ourselves as to our own motivations and ultimate objectives in evangelism. This provides a personal authenticity that is very quickly and deeply impressed on the mind of our neighbor, often based on our nonverbal communication. The neighbor we have selected may be asking, "How do you really want me to respond?" Or the question may really be, "Why do you seem to care so much about me? What is your hidden agenda? What are you really after?"

In other words, what are the ultimate motivations and goals of your evangelistic activity? To help us see more clearly those motivations and goals that are authentically biblical, let's first consider some that are not.

1. Survival: My church is dying; we do not have enough members to pay the bills. So, even though I'd rather we remained our own little exclusive club, for the sake of our survival, I will participate in relational evangelism.

2. Projection: I think everyone is like me. Since I have found that my faith in Jesus Christ is the best thing that ever happened to me, I want to make sure everyone else experiences the same thing.

3. Messianic Triumphalism: I think I have the answer to everyone else's problems. Even if they don't ask me for my opinion, I think so highly of myself that I want to tell everyone else what to do.

4. Institutionalism: My prestige and power in the church is related to how many new people I bring into my church. The greater

the number of those who are there because of me, the more I can influence the decisions and directions of the church.

5. Fanatic Sectarianism: I view my group as the only authentically Christian one in my area, so I make every effort to pull people out of their churches and bring them into the real truth represented by my group.

Clearly, we want to stay as far away from these types of wrong-headed hidden agendas as we possibly can. Vernon Grounds has highlighted this matter by warning "Watch Your Attitude." He calls for our evangelistic effort to be a matter of "communicating confidently, communicating honestly, communicating prayerfully, communicating compassionately, and communicating incarnationally."[1]

So, then, what may be our motivation for doing careful, loving, intentional, relational evangelism? Ben Johnson discusses this matter in a very enlightening way in *Friend-Maker for God*.[2] Among other motivations, Johnson mentions the following positive motivations that we will present here in outline form. One or several of them may reflect your own perspective.

A. The needs of persons

1. People are disoriented and alone.
2. People need to find fulfillment and meaning.
3. People need God to break the hold of evil in their lives so they can experience feelings of self-worth, acceptance, and self-esteem, no matter what problems they face.

B. The glory of God

1. Evangelism fulfills God's plan to reach all people with the gospel (1 Tim. 2.4-6).
2. Evangelism fulfills God's purpose when we reach people for him (2 Cor. 6.16).
3. Evangelism fulfills God's purpose for us to come into relationship with God (John 1.10-13).

C. The commission of Jesus Christ our Lord (Matt. 28.19-20, Acts 1.8, Matt. 9.37-38)

We could add a fourth major category of motivations to those suggested above. This involves the nature of who we are as God's children, as members of the body of Christ, and as disciples of Jesus. Acts 1.8 tells us that we ARE witnesses, 2 Corinthians 5.20 tells us that we ARE ambassadors, and 1 Peter 2.5 informs us that we ARE being built up to be a holy temple. In other words, evangelism is at the heart of who we ARE. Evangelism arises out of our very nature as the church. One positive motivation, therefore, will emphasize that we are most truly witnesses, ambassadors, and disciples when we are intentionally and concretely engaged in evangelism.[3]

What is your motivation for participating in evangelism? What is the strongest reason for you personally to engage in an evangelistic outreach?

Our Goals in Evangelism

Another way to clarify what we mean by evangelism is to examine what our goals might be. Peter's hearers asked, "What shall we do?" We ask ourselves, "If we had our way, what is the result we seek in our evangelistic efforts?" This is probably the most difficult matter for any of us to grasp regarding evangelism. In fact, there has been sustained debate about the goal of evangelism since the Church of England offered its definition of evangelism in 1918. It was said then that evangelism is "So to present Jesus Christ in the power of the Holy Spirit, that (people) SHALL come to put their trust in God through Him, to accept Him as their Saviour, and serve Him as their King in the fellowship of His Church."[4] In 1961 British theologian J. I. Packer suggested that the word "shall" ought to be changed to "may" in order to define evangelism in terms of purpose rather than of result. So Packer offered this definition of evangelism:

> According to the New Testament, evangelism is just preaching the gospel, the evangel. It is a work of communication in which Christians make themselves mouthpieces of God's message of mercy to sinners. . . . The way to tell whether in fact you are evangelizing is not to ask whether conversions are known to have resulted from your witness. It is to ask whether you are faithfully making known the gospel message.[5]

Packer's emphasis is echoed in *Evangelism in Reformed Perspective: An Evangelism Manifesto*, a marvelous and very helpful document jointly produced by the Reformed Church in America and the Christian Reformed Church. This document affirms that

> To evangelize is to proclaim the good news of God's reign. The sense of public proclamation is always dominant in the biblical use of the term. . . . We affirm, accordingly, that all evangelizing in the New Testament sense of the term includes the joyous proclamation of God's saving rule, together with the call to repent and believe the gospel (Acts 20.21).[6]

In the 1980s C. Peter Wagner, following Donald McGavran, vehemently opposed J. I. Packer's change of the word "shall" to the word "may." The contention of Wagner and McGavran was that the goal of evangelism is not achieved simply by proclamation. True biblical evangelism, for them, includes the matter of seeing that the hearers accept Jesus Christ and are incorporated into the church. As Wagner saw it,

> Packer has touched the heart of the problem. Is evangelism merely preaching the gospel so that many hear, or does it go further and insist on bringing the hearers into a personal relation-

ship with Christ? . . . Proclamation evangelism measures success against the yardstick of how many people hear and understand the gospel message. . . . Persuasion evangelism evaluates success only in terms of how many new disciples are made, how many persons previously without Christ and without hope in this world commit their lives to him and become members of the household of God.[7]

Packer's and Wagner's perspectives on the goal of evangelism affect the way they would evaluate their activity. Packer and many others would evaluate evangelism on the basis of the degree to which the gospel has been proclaimed. Wagner, on the other hand, would evaluate evangelism on the basis of the RESULTS, in terms of the number of those who in fact become disciples of Jesus Christ and responsible members of the church.

It is a matter of record that both J.I. Packer and C. Peter Wagner found themselves quite sympathetic to a mediating position articulated by Michael Green in *Evangelism and the Early Church*. Green defined evangelism as "proclaiming the good news of salvation to men and women with a view to their conversion to Christ and incorporation in his church."[8] This definition would evaluate the evangelistic task in terms of the INTENTION of the evangelist, rather than in terms of the results.

A new way of looking at the matter has recently been offered by William Abraham: "We can best improve our thinking on evangelism by conceiving it as that set of intentional activities which is governed by the goal of initiating people into the kingdom of God for the first time."[9]

What makes Abraham's proposal so fascinating is that it is in fact oriented to results, but those results are not as church-centric, visible, and pragmatic as Wagner's. On the other hand, Abraham's definition avoids the danger of seeing evangelism as only verbal activity that has no specific intention of seeing the hearers converted and ultimately incorporated into the church.

DISCUSSION

Now it is your turn to give this matter some thought. Do you remember the Gospel from the Air Mission? Was I evangelized that day? As you read this chapter, how did that evangelistic approach strike you in terms of relational evangelism? In terms of your own goals, what do you really expect and desire your neighbor to do?

1. Give some thought individually to the issue of the motivations and goals of evangelism during the week prior to the discussion of this chapter. Maybe it would be helpful for each person to write a one-page definition of evangelism. That one-page definition should be in two parts: a) What are my personal motivations for being involved in relational evangelism? and b) How would I write a

definition of evangelism that states clearly my goals for being involved in relational evangelism?

2. When the group gathers, the leader may want to subdivide the group into twos and threes. Then ask each small group to do the following exercise:

a. Read together Matthew 28.16-20.

b. Look at this passage from the point of view of defining evangelism. The following outline may help you think through the implications of the passage.

The Great Commission Viewed as a Definition of Evangelism

The justification for evangelism: "All authority in heaven and on earth has been given to me"

The imperative for evangelism: "Go therefore"

The goal of evangelism: "and make disciples"

The content of evangelism: "baptizing . . . teaching"

The promise of evangelism: "I am with you always"

The time of evangelism: "to the end of the age"

c. As a small group, restate in your own words what each of these phrases may mean in terms of the motivations and goals of evangelism.

3. Finally, the leader may wish to invite the whole group to examine again the pattern of evangelism in Acts 2.

Notice that in Acts 2 the event of evangelization begins with the disciples' presence among the people, followed by their personal witness and proclamation. But it does not stop there. It proceeds to call for a response from the hearers, then to incorporate them into the church, and ultimately to impact the surrounding community. The group may want to consider the following question: Does Luke intend to give us the complete picture of what biblical evangelism is? Does he separate evangelism from incorporation, church life, and environmental impact—or are all of these part of Luke's definition of evangelism? In other words, does Luke's description of evangelism stop at verse 36? At verse 38? At verse 41? Or at verses 46-47?

ACTION

1. It might be helpful for the members of your evangelism group to contact other members of your church and ask for their viewpoints on this matter. How do other church members define evangelism? What do they consider to be appropriate motivations for doing evangelism? What do they feel are acceptable goals of evangelism? Sounding out other members of the church may help to indicate ways in which the evangelism group may be able to motivate and mobilize your church in evangelizing the unchurched in your context.

2. The members of your evangelism group should not forget to continue their prayer times, as specified in earlier chapters. It is

absolutely essential to anoint this entire activity with prayer during the duration of this study. Very little will come of this process without sustained intercession for each other, for each one's "neighbor," and for the Holy Spirit's intervention in the process. Only through prayer do we prepare ourselves to examine our own motivations and goals in evangelism, and to appropriately participate with the Spirit in this wonderful adventure of being used to bring God's presence to bear in the life of another.

[1] Vernon Grounds, "Watch Your Attitude," *Christianity Today* (XXX:18. Dec. 12, 1986), pp. 32-33.

[2] Ben Johnson, *Friend-Maker for God* (Decatur, Georgia: CTS Press, 1985), p. 11.

[3] See Charles Van Engen, *God's Missionary People: Rethinking the Purpose of the Local Church* (Grand Rapids: Baker, 1991).

[4] J.I. Packer refers to this definition in "What is Evangelism?" in H. Conn, edit., *Theological Perspectives on Church Growth* (Nutley, New Jersey: Presbyterian and Reformed. 1976), p. 98.

[5] J.I. Packer, *Evangelism and the Sovereignity of God* (London: InterVarsity Press, 1961), p. 41.

[6] The document was jointly published by the *Banner* and the *Church Herald*: Grand Rapids, 1977. The above quotation is from page 2.

[7] C. Peter Wagner, *Frontiers in Mission Strategy* (Chicago: Moody, 1971), pp. 128 and 132-133.

[8] Michael Green, *Evangelism and the Early Church* (Grand Rapids: Eerdmans, 1970), p. 7. Green's view can be found earlier in the way the Berlin Congress on Evangelism defined the term in 1966. See Carl Henry and Stanley Mooneyham, edits., *One Race, One Gospel, One Task*, Vol. 1 (Minneapolis: World Wide Pub., 1967), p. 6.

[9] William Abraham, *The Logic of Evangelism* (Grand Rapids: Eerdmans, 1989), p. 95.

CHAPTER SEVEN

Experiencing the Holy Spirit's Role in Conversion

(Acts 2.38-40)

Up to this point we have emphasized the intentionality of your role as the witness in directing your attention to your neighbor, listening to your neighbor, crafting an appropriate message, and clarifying your own goals and motivations. Parallel with these matters, we have also made a case that your intentional activity must be bathed in prayer. We are now at a point where we need to develop some of the reasons for stressing this second matter, for these reasons have to do with the role of the Holy Spirit in the conversion process.

In John chapters 14-17 Jesus promised that his departure would be followed by the coming of the Advocate (or Comforter), the Holy Spirit. This promise seems to have referred primarily to Pentecost, as it is recorded in Acts 2. However, the Acts 2 event was part of a larger pattern, exemplified by the four "pentecosts" recorded in Acts (4.31, 8.17, 10.44-46, 19.6). This is coupled with a strong emphasis in the rest of the New Testament on the continual presence, inspiration, guidance, and transforming power of the Holy Spirit in the church. The Holy Spirit's work always seems to surprise us, to stretch the limits of our normal expectations, and to point us in directions we have never considered before.

That happened to me a few years back as I listened to the conversion story of Humberto, a bricklayer living in the city of Tapachula, in southern Mexico. We were standing outside his small one-room house with split bamboo walls, tin roof, and dirt floor, located at the outskirts of town. Quietly Humberto began telling me his story.

"I have a good trade and have seldom been out of work," he said. "But my way of life was like that of everyone else around here." He waved his arm to include all the other shacks in this new housing tract. "Once I got off work on Friday afternoons, I would head for the local cantina (bar). I would then begin drinking with my friends, consuming anything alcoholic I was served. I would drink myself into a drunken stupor and stay drunk until the early morning hours of Monday. Sometime Sunday night my wife and children would try to get me home so I could sleep it off in time to go to work. Each week my wife would try to get enough money from me to be able to feed the children for the next week.

"But, Chuck, you won't believe what happened to me four weeks ago! You know Idolina, the woman from your church who is building a small house in our neighborhood, and who has been witnessing of her faith to us for the last year? Well, quite a while ago she came over to talk to me in the middle of the week when I was sober. She spoke to me and my family about the Bible and God's love. She told us about the forgiveness that Jesus offers and the change that Jesus can do in our lives. I asked her many questions, but did not ask the one I really wanted to—could Jesus free me from my alcoholism? At that time I told her I had enjoyed our conversation, but I was not interested in what she had to offer."

I listened, fascinated by Humberto's story. My curiosity was especially piqued because Idolina had invited me to give a Bible study in Humberto's home. "So," I asked, "what happened to bring about such a change in your life?"

"Well, Chuck, you may find this hard to believe, but four weeks ago, on a Saturday night, I was stone drunk. I ended up lying inside that house over there." Humberto pointed to the shell of a house under construction, with the walls up, but no doors, windows, or floor.

"In the middle of the night, in that drunken sleep, I was suddenly awakened by a very bright light in the room. A deep, deep sense of calmness, love, and acceptance came over me—like nothing I had ever felt in my life. In spite of the humid heat of the night I felt a wonderfully refreshing coolness in the room. I sat up against the wall and I saw someone standing in front of me, someone who shone like white light. Somehow I seemed to have asked that person who he was.

"I am Jesus,' he said. 'I am the one Idolina has been telling you about. I am here to heal you from your alcoholism, if you want to be healed. I am the Savior of the world.' "

Humberto looked at me with tears shining in his eyes.

"Chuck, I gave my life to Jesus that night. I couldn't go back to sleep. I discovered that I was suddenly completely sober, with a peace and inner strength that I had never known. My first reaction was to wonder how my wife and children were. I went home and woke them up to tell them the story. We spent the rest of that night praying and reading the Bible that Idolina had given us.

"I have been healed of my alcoholism. I have not touched a drop for the last four weeks. I have no desire to do so, in spite of the harassment I have received from my drinking buddies. I have more money each weekend than I ever imagined I'd have. I have stopped beating my wife, and my children are back in school. Chuck, I am a changed man. Now I want to learn everything I can about the Bible and about being a Christian, so I can explain to others what the gospel is all about."

I had the joy over the next several years of watching Humberto grow. I saw him the first day he brought his whole family to the Presbyterian church in Tapachula. His wife was wearing a new dress, and she had no bruises on her face. Her long, shiny, jet-black hair encircled like a halo a smiling face of joy and peace. Every one of the children had new clothes.

I was there the day Humberto, his wife, and all his children were called from their pew to the platform of that church, and were baptized after Humberto told the church his story. We all wept and laughed together that day. Not long after that, Humberto brought his brother, sister-in-law, and all their children to church.

It was about that time that I was again invited to give a Bible study in Humberto's home. I stood alone and silent for a moment outside that same bamboo-and-tin house, listening to the singing that came from inside and marveling over the story I had heard so many months before. Then I stepped into a small living room filled to overflowing with over fifty people—all of whom had come to know Jesus Christ through the witness of Humberto.

EXPOSITION

Not all of us have a story quite as dramatic as Humberto's. But all of us who are in the church are called to experience conversion in one way or another. Maybe if we allow the pattern of Acts 2 to open our eyes to the working of the Holy Spirit, we will gain new insight into our own conversion stories. Please read Acts 2.38-40.

In answer to the question, "What shall we do?" Peter responds: "Repent, and be baptized every one of you in the name of Jesus Christ so that your sins may be forgiven; and you will receive the gift of the Holy Spirit. For the promise [the name for the Holy Spirit in this first part of Acts] is for you, for your children, and for all who are far away—everyone whom the Lord our God calls to him" (vss. 38-39).

Peter's call for conversion, repentance, baptism, and incorporation is not much different from that of John the Baptist (Matt. 3.1-12, Mark 1.4-8) and of Jesus (Matt. 4.17, Mark 1.15). The content of the conversion of Peter's hearers is that Jesus Christ is Lord (Acts 2.36). The context of their conversion is repentance and baptism as a sign of turning from a dependence on their own righteousness as Jews to casting themselves on God's mercy, based on God's grace in Jesus Christ (vs. 38a). The inner core of their conversion is to receive the gift of the presence of the Holy Spirit in their personal, family, and corporate lives (vss. 38b, 39). The process of their conversion involves baptism in the name of Jesus Christ and incorporation into the new community of disciples (vs. 38a). The resulting experience of their conversion is a deep sense of having their sins forgiven—an experience which adherence to the Jewish law could never give, as Paul later would develop in Romans and Galatians. This conversion is for ALL WHOM THE LORD OUR GOD WILL CALL.

The operation of the Holy Spirit is intimately related to all that Peter says to his hearers. Based on what Jesus had told the disciples, Peter knows that it is the Holy Spirit's role to "prove the world wrong about sin and righteousness and judgment" (John 16.8). In the following years it would be Peter's experience to discover what Paul would explain so clearly in Philippians 2.13, "for it is God who is at work in you, enabling you both to will and to work for his good pleasure." So Luke, in writing the second chapter of Acts, wants his readers to clearly recognize the role of the Holy Spirit who is the instrument of the Lord's calling (vs. 39), of bringing about a desire on the part of the hearers to accept Peter's message (vs. 41a), and of adding these new converts to the number of the disciples (vs. 41b) as they were being saved through the Holy Spirit (vs. 47). The essence of conversion is a turning away from one's own reaching for God through searching, and yielding to God's search for that person through the Holy Spirit. Conversion is not a discovery of the hidden mysteries of the divine—that is a Hindu and New Age concept which is unbiblical and anti-Christian.[1] Rather, conversion is a recognition of one's own helplessness (addiction, in modern terms), an acknowledgment of the need for radical change, the willingness to allow the Spirit to turn one around in a totally new direction, and an openness to the Spirit's complete transformation of who we are.

When we understand the radical nature of true biblical conversion, it will become clear that none of us can save our neighbors. As much as we might like to, we cannot convince them, move them, cajole them, or manipulate them into salvation. We are only participants in a larger process, the chief agent of which is the Holy Spirit. This is why prayer is so very important in this process. Through prayer we recognize our dependence on the Holy Spirit's work, we open ourselves to being used more effectively by the Holy Spirit, and we give the situation over into the hands of Jesus Christ who, by the

Spirit, may bring about conversion in the heart of our neighbor.

This emphasis is especially important because it preserves us from proselytism and manipulation. Evangelism is not a matter of winning someone over to think like we do or of convincing someone to subscribe to the propositions we accept. Neither is evangelism a way of hooking people into supporting our particular church or our favorite agenda. Neither is our witness ultimately an effort to make our churches grow. Rather, our witness becomes one of several means through which the Holy Spirit works in the life of our neighbor to call that person to conversion, repentance, faith, baptism, and incorporation into the church. Such a conversion process is clearly spelled out in Matthew 28.16-20 and was faithfully followed by the early church, as we see it described in Acts.

REFLECTION

Our perceptions of what "conversion" means is heavily influenced by our personal faith pilgrimages. The Bible seems to encourage us to consider conversion from a wide variety of perspectives. Your evangelism study group might find it helpful to study together the matter of conversion in the lives of various biblical characters, as given below. Notice especially that there appears to be no set pattern for the way conversion occurs in the lives of these persons.

Conversion in the Lives of Biblical Women and Men

Sarai / Sarah

The victim of her husband's deceit (Gen. 12.10-20)
Manipulates how Abraham may have a son (Gen. 16.1-16)
God covenants with her to be mother of nations (Gen. 17.15-22)
Her name is changed because of God's covenant (Gen. 17.15)
Sarah laughs about the promise of having a son (Gen. 18.9-15)
Sarah gives birth to Isaac (Gen. 21.1-7)
Sarah is buried in the cave at Machpelah (Gen. 23)

Miriam

Cares for Moses, her baby brother (Exod. 2.1-10)
Sings and dances a theology of the Exodus (Exod. 15.20-21)
Struck with leprosy for rebelling against Moses (Num. 12)
Dies (Num. 20.1)

Rahab

Hides the Israelite spies because of her faith (Josh. 2.1-21)
Appears in the litany of the people of faith (Heb. 11.31)
Is recognized by James for her faith (James 2.25)
Appears in Jesus' genealogy as the mother of Boaz (Matt. 1.5)

Others:

Deborah, Ruth, Hannah, Abigail, the Shunamite Woman, Esther, the Shulamite Woman of Song of Songs, Elizabeth, Mary the mother of Jesus, Mary, Martha, Mary Magdalene, the woman accused of committing adultery, Lydia, Priscilla. Others?

Abram/Abraham
Called out (Gen. 12.1-9)
Meets Melchizedek (Gen. 14.17-24)
Receives the covenant promises (Gen. 15)
Receives the covenant sign and name change (Gen. 17)
Is willing to offer Isaac in sacrifice (Gen. 22.1-19)

Moses
An Israelite mother cares for him (Exod. 2.1-10)
Meets the Lord (YHWH) at the burning bush (Exod. 3)
Exercises fantastic powers in Egypt (Exod. 7-14)
Meets YHWH again on Mt. Sinai (Exod. 19-34)
Forbidden to enter the land for striking the rock (Num. 20.1-13)
Lifts bronze snake for healing (Num. 21.1-9)
Final address to Israel (Deut. 1-33)

Elijah
Against the Baals (1 Kings 18)
Under the juniper tree, wishing to die (1 Kings 19.1-10)
Meets YHWH at Mt. Horeb (1 Kings 19.11-18)
Rides the chariot of fire (2 Kings 2.1-13)

Jonah
Called to go to Nineveh but tries to run away (Jon. 1)
Surrenders to God's will from inside the fish (Jon. 2)
Meets a worm (Jon. 4.6-11)

Simon/Peter
Called (Matt. 4.18-22)
Commissioned (Matt. 10)
Discipled by Jesus in walking on the water (Matt. 14.22-23)
Confesses his faith in Jesus the Christ (Matt. 16.13-20)
Experiences the transfiguration (Matt. 17.1-13)
Denies his faith (Matt. 26.69-75)
Called by Jesus to feed Christ's sheep (John 21.15-19)
Preaches his Pentecost sermon (Acts 2.14-42)
Is transformed through a vision in Joppa (Acts 10)
Spirited from jail (Acts 12.1-19)

Saul/Paul
Participates in the stoning of Stephen (Acts 7.54-8.3)
The Damascus Road experience (Acts 9.1-19)
Name change during first missionary journey (Acts 13.9)
Macedonian vision (Acts 16.6-10)
The jail in Philippi (Acts 16.16-40)
Renewal/encouragement by vision (Acts 18.5-11)
Again, renewal/encouragement by vision (Acts 23.6-11)
A heavenly experience (2 Cor. 12.1-5)
Thorn in the flesh, strength in weakness (2 Cor. 12.6-10)

Others:
David (Ps. 51), Nebuchadnezzar (Dan. 3-4), Hosea, Isaiah (Isa.

6), John Mark, James and John ("sons of thunder"), and many others.

As you can see from a quick review of the spiritual pilgrimages of some of these biblical characters, no two journeys were the same; and the style, process, and type of conversion experience was different in each case. As we couple our own experience of conversion with our review of biblical examples, we might come to understand conversion as a moment, a process, a transformation, and a deepening perception. Briefly, I want to highlight some strengths and weaknesses of each way of looking at conversion.

1. Conversion as a Moment

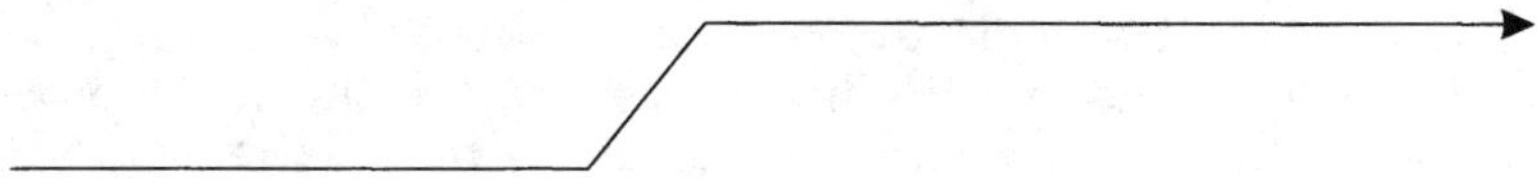

For some people, conversion comes as an identifiable, life-changing moment of transformation when they experience as never before the presence, forgiveness, and complete reorientation of the way they look at themselves, at their values, and at others around them.

The experience of Saul of Tarsus meeting Jesus on the road to Damascus is one of the most striking examples of this type of conversion. The experience of Moses at the burning bush is another. The conversion of Mary Magdalene also falls into this category.

The strength of this type of conversion experience is that it gives an identifiable moment when the person began to walk with God, a moment which provides assurance and stability in the future, a moment to which persons may later point to affirm that they have made a radical decision to follow Jesus.

The weakness of this experience is that it may simply be a moment of emotionalism, a passing fancy, with little long-range consequences. This may result in stagnation following the moment. If the moment was truly life-transforming, the temptation is to project this moment as a basis for judging the validity of the conversion or "spirituality" of others.

2. Conversion as a Series of Encounters with God

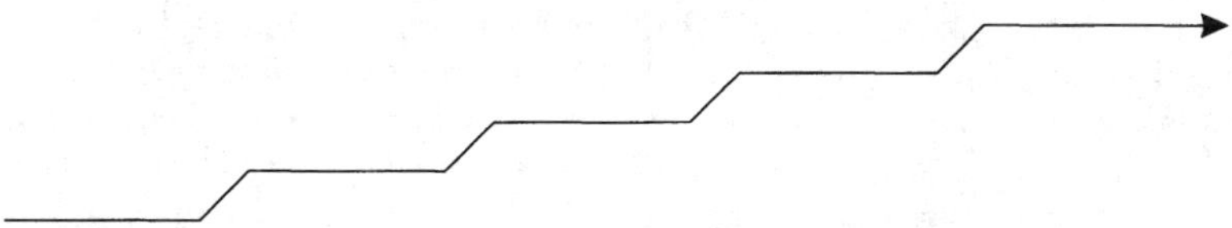

Other people experience conversion as a series of encounters with God. They can speak of identifiable moments, yet stress that these moments have been in the plural. People with this experience emphasize that each moment by itself may not have been as life-changing and transformational as the first type. But these people also testify that the cumulative effect of all those smaller moments has been as radically transformational as the one-moment experience.

Peter is a good example of this type of conversion. When Peter confessed Jesus as Lord, when he was commissioned to feed Jesus' sheep, and when he was called to go to Cornelius, he was experiencing a series of conversion encounters. The spiritual pilgrimage of Mary and Martha also looks like a series of significant spiritual encounters.

The strength of this type of conversion experience is the realization that God at specific times calls us back to a growing and developing relationship with him. The series of moments helps the Christian to continually seek to renew his or her relationship with God, rather than remain focused on one moment in the distant past.

But this kind of conversion has its weaknesses as well. The "low" points between encounters with God may imply that one is caught in a never-ending cycle of guilt and grace, without living out the life of gratitude that continually grows in intimacy with God and freedom in the Spirit.

3. Conversion as a Process

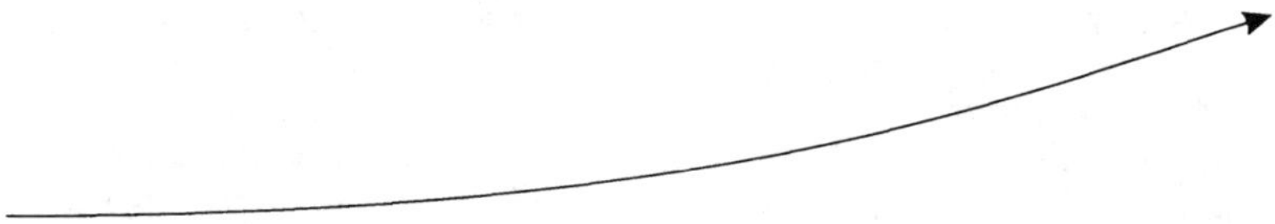

Many second- and third-generation Christians tend to speak of conversion as a process. Their grandparents were Christians, their parents were Christians, and maybe they never really questioned whether they themselves were Christians. They cannot tell you the day or the hour in which they became Christians. They may not even be able to identify major moments when they were significantly impacted by the presence of God. Yet they know that there has been a gradual progress in their understanding of faith and a developing growth in closeness to Jesus Christ.

There is a sense in which John Mark's story fits this pattern. Ruth the Moabite's spiritual pilgrimage also follows a similar vein. In both cases we can trace a gradual maturing over time, but cannot find one or several major transforming moments. It may be that our "neighbor" is in a conversion process similar to this—and that we are a small part of that larger spiritual pilgrimage.

The strength of this perspective is that it reflects accurately the experience of many who have grown up in a Christian home where infant baptism and covenant theology were taken seriously. Often these people cannot point to a moment, or even to a series of moments, that seem to be major turning points in their lives with God.

Here, too, there is a weakness. Persons experiencing conversion as a process may doubt their salvation, especially as they compare themselves to those who have experienced conversion as a major transforming moment. Unlike those who can name the day and hour, these persons may not be able to identify a time of radical conversion. The Christian life may become more a matter of Christian culture, Christianization, or behavior-modification, than an encounter with God.

4. Conversion as a Deepening Perception

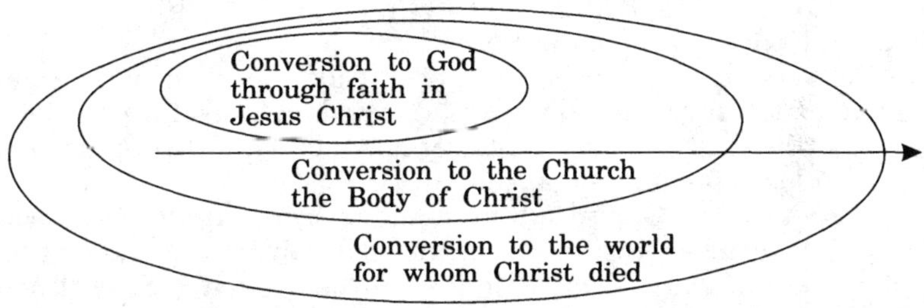

Finally, there are those who will express dissatisfaction with the whole idea of pilgrimage or journey. They will not speak of coming from someplace or going somewhere. Rather, they speak of their spiritual development in terms of deepening, of greater understanding, and of increasing fullness of the sense of God's presence. Mary the mother of Jesus pondered all her experiences "in her heart" (Luke 2.19). She seems to have grown in her understanding of Jesus' messianic role throughout his ministry, death, resurrection, and ascension. And her experience of Pentecost deepened her wisdom even more. Barnabas' development also seemed to follow this pattern, as did that of Joseph.

The strength of this viewpoint is that it demonstrates the relationship of personal conversion to God, to other individuals, to the church, to the kingdom of God, and to the world. This is an activist view of conversion, one that is constantly seeking deeper understanding of God's will for the person in relation to the world.

The weakness of this concept is that conversion and personal piety can become matters to be judged on the basis of a person's participation in social transformation, regardless of that individual's personal relationship with Jesus Christ.

As you reflect on the various forms which conversion may take in the lives of people, it is important that you realize that conversion is *not a decision to go to church*. Essentially, conversion speaks of the work of the Holy Spirit in the life of an individual, a work that has to do with that person's covenantal relationship with God and the implications of that relationship for the person's perception and behavior in relation to self, others, and the world. Lesslie Newbigin has given us some wise counsel in seeking to understand conversion:

> If the reading of history and the actual experience of converts is our guide, we shall learn that there is no direct proportion between evangelistic effort and resulting conversion. Over and over again the massive campaign produces nothing, and some quiet word spoken in the ordinary course of a caring human relationship is the seed that produces a mighty harvest. . . . Conversion is a miraculous work of God. . . . It is by his calling that the paradigm shift occurs which makes the story of the cross the power of God to salvation.[2]

Stephen Neill is also helpful here:

> Conversion is to Christ. It is primarily and essentially a personal event in which a human person is laid hold of by the living Jesus Christ at the very center of his being and turned towards him in loving trust and obedience . . .
>
> Conversion to Christ is therefore also commitment to be with him and with all who are so committed in continuing in the power of the same anointing, proclaiming, and bearing. It is commitment to follow Jesus, with all who are so committed, along the way of the cross—the way of fearless and trustful encountering and enduring the power of evil in the contemporary world.[3]

E. Stanley Jones views conversion a little differently. He says that

> Conversion is a gift and an achievement. It is the act of a moment and the work of a lifetime. You cannot attain salvation by discipline—it is the gift of God. But you cannot retain it without disciplines. . . . Discipline is the fruit of conversion—not the root. . . .
>
> There is no experience of conversion which will make you immune against the lack of reading of the Word of God and prayer. When prayer fades out, power fades out. We are as spiritual as we are prayerful, no more, no less.[4]

Jones has also given us some very helpful suggestions as to how we may cultivate the impact that our conversion can have on our lives. We are primarily concerned in this section, you may remember, with the nature of conversion and how that impacts our view of our own and our neighbor's spiritual pilgrimage. You may find, however, that the following suggestions serve not only to help you cultivate your conversion, but also to understand more clearly what it is. Here, then, are Stanley Jones' suggestions for cultivating the impact of conversion in our spiritual journeys:

1. Cultivate the new life by daily disciplines.
2. Keep honest at any cost.

3. Keep confessing your sins after conversion.

4. Pray for those who have wronged you.

5. Constantly enlarge the area of your conversion. Make your conversion take in more and more areas of your life.

6. Give up habits that cannot be Christianized.

7. After partaking of the divine nature, add these things:

> "His divine power has granted to us all things that pertain to life and godliness . . . and become partakers of the divine nature. For this very reason make every effort to supplement your faith with virtue, and virtue with knowledge, and knowledge with self-control, and self-control with steadfastness, and steadfastness with godliness, and godliness with brotherly affection, and brotherly affection with love" (2 Pet. 1.3-7, RSV).

8. Fix the habit of tithing your income.

9. Don't wait for the big tasks; do the little ones in a big way.

10. Make it a habit to repeat every night before you drop off to sleep the words, "In him who strengthens me, I am able for anything."

11. Live in a state of relaxed receptivity.

12. Form the habit of speaking to somebody every day about Christ.[5]

DISCUSSION

A rewarding, stimulating, and inspirational experience is for an evangelism group to take about a half hour and listen to each other tell conversion stories. The leader may want to organize everyone into groups of three or four, so that each person can have about ten minutes to speak of her or his experience of conversion. Remember that there are various types of conversion experiences. The guidelines that follow may help facilitate this sharing time.

1. As the Spirit moves (always give anyone who wishes the option of NOT telling their story), have the members of each group tell about an experience that felt to them like "conversion."

2. In the telling of their personal experiences, it might be helpful for the members of the group to reflect on whether their own pilgrimages look like conversion as a moment, as a series of moments, as a process, or as a deepening consciousness of God's presence—and what may be the implications for their spiritual journeys.

3. Allow some time for the small groups to discuss the implications of their conversion stories on their communication of the gospel with their neighbor. Should they expect their neighbor to mirror their own particular experience of conversion?

ACTION

Our personal experience of conversion inevitably colors the way we witness to our neighbor and what our expectations may be regarding our neighbor's conversion.

1. Each member of your evangelism group should take some time during the coming week to write a one-page description of the implication of "conversion" for their neighbor. Again, reflect on the complementary aspects of conversion as a moment, a series of moments, a process, or a deepening awareness of God's presence. What, might you guess, would be the shape and the implications of conversion if the Holy Spirit brought about such an experience in the life of your neighbor? Remember that the Holy Spirit is always full of surprises. So your guesses may or may not be the way your neighbor actually experiences conversion. At any rate, you need to be very aware that "conversion" as it impacts your neighbor's life may take a very different shape and may imply quite distinct changes from those which you have experienced. Do not project on your neighbor a need to experience the same kind of conversion you have had.

2. Please remember your prayer commitments, praying for each other in the group—especially now that you are more fully aware of what conversion was like in their experience. Pray also for your neighbor's conversion—especially now that you are aware of the breadth of possible ways in which the Holy Spirit may work in your neighbor's life.

3. During this week you may want to try to find out if your neighbor ever had some kind of conversion-type experiences, a kind of "transforming moment" when your neighbor was clearly aware of God's presence. If the occasion presents itself, share something about your own conversion experiences with your neighbor, and then ask about your neighbor's. You may be pleasantly surprised to discover a range of experiences in your neighbor's background.

[1] New Age teachings—like those about channeling, getting in touch with the mysterious forces of the divine in nature and in oneself, and tapping psychic and spiritual power—have roots in ancient first century mystery religions, in the meditation movements of the 1970s, and in a modified Hinduism. Those teachings have no room for a God who created and rules the universe. They do not accept the fact of sin, and they do not allow for redemption in Jesus Christ. They are incompatible with biblical teaching. They need to be faced squarely and to be firmly rejected as unacceptable for Christians.

[2] Lesslie Newbigin, "Context and Conversion," *International Review of Mission* (LXVIII:20, July 1979), pp. 305-306.

[3] Stephen Neill, *Open Secret* (Grand Rapids: Eerdmans, 1978), pp. 156-157.

[4] E. Stanley Jones, *Conversion* (New York: Abingdon, 1959), taken from Chapter XII, "The Cultivation of Conversion," pp. 210-217.

[5] Ibid.

CHAPTER EIGHT

Incorporating the Convert into the Congregation's Fellowship

(Acts 2.41-42)

During the last several decades, evangelists and church growth enthusiasts have emphasized the importance of the church's obedience to the great commission, as expressed in Matthew 28.18-20:

> All authority in heaven and on earth has been given to me. Go therefore and make disciples of all nations, baptizing them in the name of the Father and of the Son and of the Holy Spirit, and teaching them to obey everything that I have commanded you. And remember, I am with you always, to the end of the age.

Particularly in mass evangelism, churches have been quite intentional about obeying the "go and make disciples" part of the commission, encouraging thousands to come forward in evangelistic meetings, meet with a counselor, sign a decision card, and demonstrate a new commitment to follow Jesus Christ. Whether through individual conversions or mass movements, Christian mission has placed heavy emphasis on the matter of this initial decision to believe in Jesus Christ.

What has too often been ignored as an integral part of evangelism is the rest of the great commission. Too often we have forgotten that we are also to be involved in "baptizing them . . . and teaching them to obey everything that I have commanded you." The *baptizing* refers to incorporation into the body of Christ, and the *teaching* speaks of discipling and training the new converts so that they may become witnesses and evangelists in their own right.

EXPOSITION

Please read carefully Acts 2.41-42, taking special note of the way the incorporation of the new converts is presented as an integral part of the whole evangelistic process. There was a time when some people spoke of "pre-evangelism," "evangelism," and "post-evangelism." They separated the matters of the church's presence in the world (pre-evangelism), along with incorporation of the converts into the church (follow-up, or post-evangelism), as somehow different from the event of the communication of the gospel itself (evangelism). This perspective is clearly not shared by Luke, as he records the events of the book of Acts. Luke highlights the way in which this first group of believers lived out precisely what their Lord had commanded them. Baptism, incorporation into the church, teaching, discipleship, and subsequent continued witness by all who became part of the body—this is Luke's norm for the church. There is a natural flow from the proclamation of the gospel by Peter to the incorporation of the 3,000 new converts:

> Those who welcomed his message were baptized, and that day about three thousand persons were added. They devoted themselves to the apostles' teaching and fellowship, to the breaking of bread and the prayers (Acts 2.41-42).

Luke is presenting us with more than an account here. He is demonstrating for us a clear pattern that is followed later by Paul and is expected of the entire church: baptism, incorporation, teaching, fellowship, sacrament, and prayer. This, then, is the pattern of behavior expected of us when we bring to our church the neighbor who has expressed interest in becoming a Christian. In other words, we need to include in relational evangelism a process that naturally leads to baptizing, incorporating, teaching, discipling, and mobilizing our converted neighbor in and through the church and toward mission in the world. It is not enough to bring a new person to church, or even to bring that new person to the point of becoming a member of a church. The evangelizing process includes discipling, spiritual formation, and loving nurture of the new converts, "teaching them to obey everything that I have commanded you" (Acts 2.20).

Thus in our local churches it is not enough to create programs that develop new contacts, share Christ with the unchurched, and bring the unchurched to a decision of faith-relationship with Jesus. That, in fact, is only the beginning. The evangelization of those persons continues by "teaching them. . . . " It means that the witnesses, once they have begun to develop a faith-relationship with their neighbors, will in fact need the church's educational programs, worship experiences, small-group events, and a host of other activities to extend their witness toward discipling the convert—until the convert becomes a witness as well.

This new perspective brings new purpose, new function, and new light to all of our church programs. No longer are the church's activities to be done only "by the members, of the members, and for the members." Now the church's programs become a set of evangelistic tools whereby the new converts are taught, discipled, and equipped to become witnesses in their own right. This matter of incorporation is so important because it gives concrete expression to the most basic characteristic of the disciples of Jesus: love. Ultimately, the local congregation is nothing if it is not a loving fellowship of those who follow Jesus Christ in the power of the Holy Spirit (1 Cor. 13).

REFLECTION

The disciples of Jesus understood that "agape" love is the way of life expected of the people of God. The attitude and action of self-giving love was expected of God's people from the earliest records in the Old Testament (see Lev. 19.18 and Prov. 20.22, 24.29) In fact, Jesus considered love of God and love of neighbor as the sum total of the law (Mark 12.29-31).

Now here is one of the most crucial steps in the evangelistic process outlined for us in Acts. Up until now we have been thinking about individuals—yourself as the witness and your neighbor as the person to whom you have chosen to witness. But now it becomes more complex. Your neighbor may express a desire to attend your church either before or after experiencing conversion, and you are the most appropriate person to introduce your neighbor to your church.

As you know, when someone becomes a new member of a woman's club or is invited to join a chapter of Rotary International, that person is often sponsored by another person who is already a member. When the time comes for the new candidate to meet everyone, the sponsor comes along with the new member, introduces the new member to the others, and explains the procedures of the club to the new member.

Why do we expect anything less in the church? Who are we to think that we have welcomed a prospective member by letting that person come to our church by themselves, not being greeted by anyone, not knowing anyone, sitting alone during the worship service, and not receiving a cordial handshake upon leaving? What leads us to believe that there is any reason for that person to return?

The type of relational evangelism we have been envisioning must necessarily involve you in the process of incorporating your neighbor into the life of the congregation. I hope that the congregation will organize a series of events that will give you the opportunity to invite your neighbor to attend. When this happens, I hope that you will extend the invitation to your neighbor and make arrangements to go to church together. I hope that you will walk in together and that you will immediately begin introducing your neighbor to other members of the church. I hope that during the program you will sit together, and that afterward you will again seek out opportunities to introduce your neighbor to other members of your church.

To make this process work, we need to reflect on the various ways in which a congregation can help you incorporate the new convert. Especially, we need to consider all the various entry points at which your neighbor might possibly become part of the life of your congregation.

In *Who Cares About Love?* Win and Charles Arn published the results of a very interesting study they conducted. They surveyed a substantial number of congregations, asking old and new members whether they felt that their congregation was a loving one. Sadly, many mainline congregations came in near the bottom of the list, as not being very loving.[1]

Unfortunately too many of our church activities and programs are carried out by the members, for the members, responding to the agendas of the members. Youth groups, Sunday school classes, couples' clubs, small care groups, and even Stephen's Ministries are too often oriented to serving those who are already part of the church. What is needed is to look carefully at every primary group in the church and to ask whether any of them may serve as entry points for your neighbor to become familiar with the church and to get acquainted with the members of your church.

In his *Evangelism Primer* Ben Johnson talks about "organismic evangelism" as a way of describing this kind of evangelistically-oriented programming in a congregation that intentionally structures itself for incorporating new converts:

> I have chosen the word "organismic" to define the kind of evangelism that stems from the understanding of the church I have set forth (the people of God and the body of Christ). An organism is a complex structure of interdependent and subordinate elements whose relations and functions are largely determined by their relation to the whole. "Organismic evangelism" is, therefore, a complex structure of being, doing, and telling the "good news"; its interrelationships are largely determined by the evangelistic imperative to the whole body of Christ: "to make disciples of all nations."[2]

Ben Johnson is making a point about the commitment of the whole congregation to incorporate and disciple new converts. He calls on the members of the congregation to look at their own motivations and priorities. How important is it to the entire organism that new people be incorporated and discipled in and through the programs of the church? This question must be asked of *all* the various programs of the church. It needs to be studied to see if a deep commitment to incorporating new members permeates the entire life of the organism. Without such a commitment, the congregation will not grow. Ben Johnson calls for analyzing the "climate" of the congregation from the point of view of such a commitment:

> If the worship of a congregation lacks life, if the church has no clear identity, if factions reign, if persons are unconcerned about outsiders, if the minister has grown insensitive to the pain of the congregation, if the congregation ignores the needs of the community, and if the church primarily serves the needs of its members, that church has a sick climate, not a climate for growth. . . .
>
> The congregation's attitude toward growth affects the climate for evangelism. If a church does not want to grow, it will not grow. Nearly all churches state verbally their desire to grow. Often, however, their profession means, "We want to grow if persons will conform to the traditions and values of the church, but we do not want to grow if it requires change." A church unwilling to change (for the sake of the newcomers) is a church resistant to growth.
>
> Cultivation of prospective members must begin immediately upon their contact with the church. Every week that passes after a prospective member's first visit to the church reduces the likelihood of that person joining the church by 50 percent. Experience demonstrates repeatedly that the faster the church responds to the visitor, the more likely that person is to become a regular participant in that church.[3]

Peter Wagner echoes Johnson's view by showing us the difference between *koinonia* and "koinonitis" (an inflammation of the *koinonia*):

> *Koinonia* is the biblical word for fellowship, a prominent Christian virtue. The Christians in that vigorous, healthy church in Jerusalem were characterized, among other things, by *koinonia* (Acts 2.42). . . . Providing appropriate structures for fellowship to occur is essential for healthy church growth. When these are either nonexistent or when they become inoperative for some reason or other, the church fails to grow. Maladies which affect the fellowship dynamics of the church fall into the general category of koinonitis. . . .
>
> Fellowship, by definition, involves interpersonal relationships. It happens when Christian believers get to know one another, enjoy one another, and care for one another. But as the disease develops, and *koinonia* becomes koinonitis, these interpersonal relationships become so deep and so mutually absorbing, they can provide the focal point for almost all church activity and involve-

> ment. Church activities and relationships become (introverted). . . .
>
> The reason for this is that somewhere in the process of developing the disease, the focus on the church's philosophy becomes "us." The church exists for itself and its members and not for those who are outside the fellowship. The people within the church have been reconciled to God, and they love each other. Who cares about those outside?[4]

There was a time when I was youth pastor of a small congregation in Pasadena, California. When I began my work there, I discovered that there were a substantial number of young single adults who had at one time been related to that church, but who were no longer to be seen. They were somewhere in the woodwork, known to other members of the church, but not involved in any way in the life of the congregation.

So I began a concerted effort to get to know them, gather them together, and help them to get to know each other. I stressed heavily the development of mutual caring, sharing, and love—and was quite successful in developing among them a vibrant and dynamic *koinonia*. Soon a number of other young singles who had not been related to the church also joined our group and became an integral part of our fellowship.

One of them we will call Sam. Sam was stationed at a nearby Air Force base and had just returned from a stint in Vietnam. He was alone, lonely, rather lost, and hungry for fellowship and acceptance. On the weekend that our group went up into the mountains for a retreat, I spoke at length with Sam as we stood in the newly-fallen snow. He spoke of his time in "Nam," of his deep searches for the presence of God and the meaning of life, and of his thirst for acceptance, friendship, and love.

Sam quickly became a key person in our group. Soon he brought his closest Air Force buddy, an artist and comic, to join us as well. Then he befriended a "hippie" and his girlfriend. They too became part of our group. Slowly we learned to trust each other, open up to each other and to God, care for each other, and depend on one another. Eventually Sam became the choir director of our church and served on the staff of another church. He is now very actively involved in another church, along with his wonderful wife, a girl who had grown up in our church and who had been instrumental in the original development of our singles group.

Unfortunately, I had not read about "koinonitis." Precisely what Peter Wagner describes happened to us in that group. I had been so absorbed by the early needs for growth in trust, intimacy, and fellowship, that I did not readjust my thinking after such a climate was created. I continued to work on developing the same type of thing and was not nearly as intentional as I should have been in developing an outward-directed, extroverted, missional perspective for the group. We neglected to find ways of reaching out to those who were not yet part of us.

I began to notice that newcomers would come to our group, meet once or twice with us, and never come again. Shortly after, I left my work at that church, and a few years later the group disbanded.

It wasn't until quite a few years later that I discovered what our mistake had been. We had been right in emphasizing fellowship and love. But soon we were loving each other too exclusively and caring for each other too closely. There was no room for newcomers. We had our inside jokes, our shared experiences, our deep understanding of each other, our common history. Any newcomer would immediately recognize that this was a family in which there was no emotional and interpersonal space for new members. The group had developed "koinonitis," a condition in which the *koinonia* became inflamed to such an extent that it began to exist predominantly "of the members, by the members, and for the members." Eventually the group (the organism) died, because it had no way of replacing itself.

Whose church is it, anyway? Does John 3.16 say, "For God so loved the *church*"? Your congregation ultimately does not exist for itself—it exists for the sake of those who are not yet part of your church. But does your church in fact live its life, structure its programs, and develop its interpersonal relationships in such a way that it actually embodies in its organismic life this kind of ultimate commitment to be a receiving fellowship with an open invitation to newcomers?

DISCUSSION

Your evangelism group can be of great assistance to the pastors, leaders, and members of your church if it does a detailed analysis of your congregation at this point. Here are some questions that some of the members of your group might want to ask.

1. What are the entry points for new converts in becoming part of the life of your congregation? What activities, groups, or meetings in your church are good opportunities to bring in new people?

2. What is the role of small care groups in your church in incorporating newcomers? Check some of the groups in your church to see if they have incorporated any new members during the last six months.

3. Interview individuals in your church who have become members during the last year. Ask them how they first became familiar with the church, what motivated them to come, what part of the church's life they first began to participate in, and what it felt like when they first began to attend. Finally, ask them in what ways the congregation has continued to incorporate, disciple, and equip them after they began attending regularly. In *Attracting New Members*, Robert Bast has provided a helpful survey that can help us understand better the needs and interests of new members.[5]

4. Now consider your neighbor in relation to your congregation.

a. Why should your neighbor be interested in coming to your church?

b. What activity, group, or part of your church's life would be the most natural entry point for your neighbor?

c. What plans do you have to invite, come with, introduce, and join with, your neighbor in the incorporation process? Are you willing to some day attend the new members' class with your neighbor?

5. Your evangelism group could obtain copies of the bulletins from the last four Sundays. You might enjoy looking at them, not for your sake, but through the eyes of your neighbor. Remember all that you learned in Chapter Four about listening to your neighbor and seeing reality through your neighbor's perspective. Now examine the bulletins and think about the organizations, programs, style and language of worship, style of leadership, topics and style of the sermons, and subject areas of study in your congregation. Do they reflect any of your neighbor's concerns? Would your neighbor understand what is going on? Would any of it speak to your neighbor's interests, agendas, and needs? If you find some that will do the above, mark them in your mind as possible entry points for the way you will begin to incorporate your neighbor into the life of your congregation. If you find almost none that satisfy these needs (and this is far more common than you might imagine), begin thinking of ways in which your congregation can change the way it does things—*for the sake of those who are not yet part of your church.*

ACTION

1. Your group may wish to assign various members to do some investigating along the lines of the above questions. One of the action steps at this point may be to gather the appropriate information that can then be reported and discussed the following week. Some members of your group may want to spend time examining all the physical, programmatic, and interpersonal aspects of your church *from the point of view of their neighbors.*

2. A few members of your church may want to interview some people with regard to the above questions. Two groups need to be surveyed. One is a number of people who began to attend your church during the last year. The second group is some of the "neighbors" chosen by the members of your evangelism group at the beginning of this study.

3. The members of your group can now commit themselves to pray for your church, for each other, and for their neighbors in terms of the incorporation of newcomers into the life of your church. If your discussion has highlighted ways in which it is urgent for your congregation to change, you will want to pray diligently and

fervently for the church to be willing to make such changes.

If in your discussion you have discovered that your congregation is not really committed to growing, this issue needs to be saturated with prayer, seeking the Holy Spirit's guidance for ways in which the members of your group may bring about that deep change in the orientation, commitment, and climate of your church. Such a commitment must permeate the entire life of the congregation, including pastors, leaders, and members. You may discover what many others have found. One of the most difficult aspects of an evangelism task force's work is bringing about necessary changes in your congregation so that it may become an incorporating organism that is receptive to newcomers.

[1] (Pasadena: Church Growth Press, 1986). See also Kennon Callahan, *Twelve Keys to an Effective Church* (New York: Harper & Row, 1983).

[2] Ben Johnson, *An Evangelism Primer: Practical Principles for Congregations* (Atlanta: John Knox, 1983), p. 27.

[3] *Ibid,* pp. 31-33, *49*.

[4] Peter Wagner, *Your Church Can Be Healthy* (Nashville: Abingdon, 1979), pp. 78-79.

[5] Robert Bast, *Attracting New Members* (New York: Reformed Church Press, 1989), p. 160.

CHAPTER NINE

Involving the Convert in Witness

(Acts 2.43-47)

Did you notice the shift we made in the last chapter? We began our study on evangelism from a strongly individualistic perspective, speaking of our spiritual journey, then about our neighbor, and then about sharing our faith with our neighbor out of the richness of that journey. But in Chapter Eight we found it necessary to change our focus from the individual to the corporate. This shift is essential, because it is to be found at the heart of the gospel. Faith in Jesus Christ is intimately related with incorporation into his body, the church, of which he is the head (Col. 1 and Eph. 4). As we come to Jesus, we are built into being part of the Temple of which he is the chief cornerstone (1 Pet. 2).

The apostle John knew this, and he structured his gospel around this idea. John begins with individuals inviting other individuals to "come and see" Jesus (1.29-51). But John then builds his gospel toward a corporate perspective as found in Jesus' prayer, "that they may be one" (17.11) and in Jesus' command to Peter, "feed my sheep" (21.17).

EXPOSITION

Luke develops his story of Pentecost along similar lines. Luke begins his narrative with a strongly individualistic perspective that emphasizes personalities: the twelve, the women, Mary the mother of Jesus, and the 120 who experience the first Pentecost (Acts 1.12-15). But watch carefully how Luke tells the rest of the story. By the time you get to the end of chapter two, Luke is no longer dealing with individuals; he is dealing with a group, a corporate community, a body:

> Awe came upon everyone, because many wonders and signs were being done by the apostles. All who believed were together and had all things in common; they would sell their possessions and goods and distribute the proceeds to all, as any had need. Day by day, as they spent much time together in the temple, they broke bread at home and ate their food with glad and generous hearts, praising God and having the goodwill of all the people. And day by day the Lord added to their number those who were being saved (Acts 2.43-47).

But I want you to notice something else. Luke describes more than the internal life of this new fellowship. He ingeniously wraps his description of the internal life of this fellowship with phrases that point us outward to the impression this fellowship was creating in its surrounding context, the city of Jerusalem. Like bookends, enclosing the life of the congregation, Luke uses two phrases to point out that "Awe came upon everyone" [outside the fellowship] (2.43), and the new fellowship was "having the goodwill of all the people" (2.47).

In other words, Luke's perspective does not deal only with the Christian fellowship. It also emphasizes the social (or sociological) impact of the fellowship upon its surrounding environment. The disciples' life together internally had an impact on the community externally—an impact that led to continued growth of the fellowship itself. Luke understood that in the final analysis the fellowship did not exist for itself; it existed for the sake of the surrounding community to which it was sent in witness. Luke wants us to see that with the coming of the Holy Spirit at Pentecost the nature of this fellowship is defined by Christ's words, "You will be my witnesses in Jerusalem, in all Judea and Samaria, and to the ends of the earth" (Acts 1.8).

There is a difference between those who are in the church and those who are not, and that difference may be thought of as a set of social, physical, emotional, personal, and spiritual boundaries. But a local congregation is not an island, and it does not exist by and for itself. It is part of a larger reality that includes all the other sociological, economic, political, relational, and religious subsystems of its surrounding context. Effective witness cannot be discovered by simply "rearranging the furniture" inside the church. Ultimately we will not impact those outside the church if we only change things inside the church. The real issue is the interaction (or, in computer language, the interface) of the congregation with its surrounding context. Luke's phrases, "Awe came upon everyone," and "having the goodwill of all the people" specifically highlight this interaction.[1]

REFLECTION

Our shift of perspective from the individual to the corporate affects the way we view the witnesses as well as how we see our neighbors. Earlier we looked at our neighbors as individuals. Now we need to begin to think of neighborhoods and communities.

The context to which your church is related consists of the sum total of several social categories. Remember that the building is not the church; the church is people. And the context in which your church exists is not the buildings, streets, or signs; it is the people who live in the houses, attend the schools, work in the businesses, and walk the streets. And the way your church responds to its surrounding context is determined by the way the members of your congregation deal with the people who are not yet in your church.

A local congregation relates to a number of different types of subsets of people in its surrounding context. Each subset is an integrated social sphere consisting of some of the people to whom your congregation relates. Your congregation is related to at least four different kinds of subsets. I have called these the relational, the programmatic, the geographic, and the new arrivals subsets.

The Relational Subset

Your church's relational subset consists of all the people impacted by your church's members in their business or work relationships, their socio-economic ties, residential neighborhoods, extended family relationships, schools, friendships, and so forth. You may recall that in Chapter Three we emphasized the various arenas of relational evangelism in terms of your natural bridges of personal relationships. Those natural bridges are multiplied by the number of members in your congregation, and you begin to see the extent of the impact your church can have on the people who come in contact with its members through normal day-to-day activities.

The families of your church constitute the most important relational bridges between your congregation and the people in the surrounding context. How your congregation ministers to its members and equips its members for ministry in the world will influence the evangelistic impact the members will have on the "neighbors" they naturally relate to in the course of their daily lives. The church's attitude can be detrimental, irrelevant, or enhancing. It is, therefore, very important to ask in what way your church is equipping and strengthening its members to witness to those persons with whom they relate during a normal week.

The Programmatic Subset

It may be that your church also impacts people who are not personally related to any member of your congregation. For example, if your church has a radio ministry, someone who otherwise would have no personal contact with your church may be impacted by the church's witness through the radio programs.

To give another example, quite a few RCA congregations have day care ministries involving children from families who do not attend the church regularly. These families are prime candidates for membership in your church and are related to the congregation through a specific program. Mid-week club programs for children, drug rehabilitation centers, counseling centers, and coffee break ministries are also examples of the kind of activities intentionally geared to provide a specific service to a certain programmatic community.

Clearly, these ministries must be of high quality. The most important question, however, is not how well they are being done, or how much money they may or may not bring in to the church. The primary question is how these ministries are providing opportunities for the church's members to build relationships with the unchurched who are being served—and what steps are being taken to invite these people to become members of the church.

It is important to look over the various programs of your church and ask who in the surrounding context are the intended recipients of these programs. Do these programs in fact reach those for whom they are intended? Do they meet the needs of that particular group of people? And are these programs structured in such a way that some of your church's members can begin to build close personal relationships that can lead to sharing their faith pilgrimages, seeking the conversion of those who are not yet Christian, and incorporating them into the church? Remember the bottom line of this evangelism study. Sooner or later, sometime, someplace, somehow, in every evangelistic effort there must be a sharing of faith between the Christian and the non-Christian in such a way that the non-Christian is confronted with the possibility of a faith-encounter with Jesus Christ—an encounter that includes incorporation into the body of Christ, the church.

It is especially important to analyze your church's programs in terms of what Harvie Conn has called "Doing Justice and Preaching Grace."[2] In Acts 2.43-47 we find no dichotomy between word and deed in the church's witness, no splitting of proclamation from demonstration. Diaconal service, personal testimony, and corporate witness go hand-in-hand in the church's programs that seek to proclaim in word, deed, and corporate life that the people of this church are the loving fellowship of the disciples of Jesus Christ.

The Geographic Subset

Have you ever noticed how often those who live next door to the building in which a congregation meets do not attend that church? One of the less effective subsets of people to which a church witnesses involves those persons who know about the church because they live somewhere near the building. Down through the centuries we can observe what may be called the "cathedral syndrome." Whenever a congregation emphasizes its building (like the churches did when they built the magnificent cathedrals that dot Europe), one can predict that the church will lower its effectiveness in reaching the *people* of its surrounding context.

The reason for this is that those who know about the church through its building tend to be unimpressed or at least uninterested in the people of the church, in their fellowship, and in the meaning of the gospel. If they are interested in the church at all, their interest will be primarily centered on the brick and mortar. The focus is wrong, the emphasis is off-center, and the message is muffled or lost. Buildings do not share their faith pilgrimage; people do. Thus church building programs tend to have a strong negative effect on relational evangelism. If a church builds a new building specifically for the sake of those who are not yet in the church, the negative impact is softened. But if the new building is the center of the congregation's attention and is being built for the sake of those who are already members (the ones who are paying the bills), relational evangelization will suffer.

The New Arrivals Subset

This is the group of people many churches seem most interested in impacting with their evangelism efforts. It is also the group of people <u>least</u> likely to produce many new converts for your church. This subset is comprised of those who happen to move into the city or town where the church is located. They end up coming to the church either because someone contacted them or because they are hunting for a church to attend.

Now remember that, biblically, our witness is from church to non-church. It is by those who are Christian to those who are not yet Christian. If a family who is new to the community begins to shop for a local church, it usually means that they have previously been members of a church in some other town. It is very important that they find a church home in the new city or town where they are now living. But the incorporation of this essentially churched family into a congregation in your town does not reduce the number of the unchurched, nor convert anyone who is not yet Christian. It only involves the recycling of the saints.

Often we look at the growth of one particular congregation (usually our own) and celebrate the fact that it is incorporating a significant number of new people. But if those people are coming from other churches, this growth is essentially irrelevant to what we are seeking here. It only recycles those who are already churched. It may be the case in your congregation that you have a pastor who is a dynamic preacher, your church is friendly and accepting, and the programs are effective. The result of such a combination may be that a significant number of people who were formerly members of other churches are now part of your church. Neither your evangelism task force nor your pastor can do much about that. You cannot simply tell these people not to come. But it is imperative that neither your church's pastoral staff nor your evangelism committee allow transfer growth to distract you from your church's primary goal: to incorporate the *unchurched*.

Some congregations are located in towns where there is a pattern of people switching churches any time a new preacher comes to town. That may be helpful for the church that receives the new ones, but it is not helpful for the churches that lose them. Even the church that receives the "church-hoppers" will discover that it cannot build a long-range future on them. The next time a new preacher comes to town, these people will move on. We need to be careful not to let transfer growth distract us from our primary goal of seeing non-Christians converted to Jesus Christ and incorporated into the church.

There is one very notable exception to the low view I have just given of evangelism related to the new arrivals subset. This exception is in contexts where there is rapid demographic change. If your area is involved in rapid population shifts, your committee needs to give serious attention to this matter. Churches in transitional neighborhoods must take seriously their commitment to reach those who are moving into the area—even if the newcomers are socio-economically or ethnically different from the present members of the church. This is a very complex matter, and we do not have space to deal with it here. There is a developing body of literature that helps older churches in transitional neighborhoods (OCTNs) take seriously the challenge of evangelizing their neighborhoods. I estimate that around half of the congregations belonging to mainline churches in North America are OCTNs.

These congregations are at least twenty-five years old, are in a survival mode, and their building is in an area of rapid social, ethnic, or economic change. This type of church is usually a commuting church, with a minority of its members living within a one-mile radius of the sanctuary. The socio-economic or ethnic makeup of the congregation is usually different from that of the people who live within a five-mile radius of the building. This type of situation has some very unique characteristics, and the congregation must do some very careful and sensitive strategic planning if it is to turn itself outward for evangelism and mission in its local context.[3] If you believe your church is an OCTN, it may be important for your evangelism task force to commit itself to additional study and prayer regarding this matter. It will, of course, eventually communicate its findings to the congregation.

Analyzing and Addressing the Various Subsets of People in Your Church's Context

There are times when the various subsets of your church's context may overlap. That is, when the same people who live near the church are neighbors, friends, or relatives of church members and are impacted by specific programs of the church. However, in many middle-urban situations (older suburban, transitional neighborhoods) where the congregation is essentially a commuting one, these four subsets do not usually inter-connect. In fact, their socio-economic, ethnic, political, and religious makeup may differ radically from one another and from the members of your congregation. The particular needs of the people that make up each of these communities may be very different, and thus the programs chosen and designed to meet those needs may vary, depending on the community being targeted.

One thing is clear. Corporate, direct, vibrant relational witness is absolutely essential, no matter which of the subsets of people is being targeted. As we said in the beginning, sooner or later there needs to be a personal witness offered by the disciples of Jesus to the ones who are not yet Christian. How that may happen varies tremendously. That it must take place is non-negotiable, if we are following the Acts 2 pattern.

During the years that my wife and I lived in Tapachula, Chiapas, Mexico, one of my most dramatic discoveries had to do with the tremendous potential of allowing the gospel to follow the natural relational bridges of the members of the church to the people of their community. Early in 1974 I met Roberto. He was an elder in the local church and made a living driving a taxi in Tapachula, a city of about 150,000. I knew that Roberto was very concerned about evangelizing his town and was very intentional about learning ways to share his faith pilgrimage with others.

But it took me several years before I began to understand the real implications of what Roberto was doing. About 1978 I noticed that three of the members of that church's men's group were taxi drivers, but that fact did not impress me very much. Then around 1982 I noticed that six of the members of the men's group drove taxis. By 1985 there were several more, and I decided it was time I asked Roberto about this. One evening after church I asked him to explain why so many taxi drivers were now members of his church.

"Oh, that. Well, brother Chuck, as you know, we all park around the center square in the middle of town, and we often have time to sit around and talk. About ten years ago, when you taught us some things about relational evangelism and how to share stories out of our personal faith pilgrimage, I decided that I would always have a Bible handy in my taxi. So during the last ten years I have prayed a lot, and have sought day after day to find ways to share my story with the other taxi drivers. I have tried never to force this matter, and I have always waited for the Holy Spirit to signal to me when to broach the subject. I have let it arise naturally in the conversation—preferably brought up by one of the other taxi drivers who is not a Christian.

"Well, you would not believe what has happened during this time. Over the years many taxi drivers have asked me about my faith and have wanted to hear the gospel. In fact, there have been occasions when we sit on our bench waiting for customers, and you would think it was a Bible study. Not all of my colleagues agree with me—in fact some are strongly opposed to me and to the gospel. But the Lord has been good. Every year at least one taxi driver has been converted by the Holy Spirit's work and has become a member of one of the churches in town. Some have come here and are members of our church. There is probably an equal number who are members of other churches. It has been my deepest joy to see my work as my ministry. Every morning I can hardly wait to get back to the town square, to sit around and talk with my colleagues, and to see which of them for whom I have been diligently praying will ask me the right question. Today is Sunday. I can hardly wait to go back to work tomorrow and see what surprises God may have in store for me."

Roberto had just given me a lesson in the way natural, unforced, intentional, and sensitive relational evangelism works as it follows our natural relational bridges. Most of us know a great deal about our webs of relationships. We need to be more intentional in allowing them to become bridges over which the love of God may be communicated to those who are not yet part of our church—the ones for whom Christ died.

DISCUSSION

1. At this point your evangelism group may want to spend at least a half hour discussing the various subsets of people with whom your church is related in its context. Identify these subsets and describe them as graphically and completely as possible. In the same way that the members of your evangelism task force learned to listen to their neighbors in Chapter Four, they can now begin to learn to listen carefully to whole groups of persons who demonstrate similar characteristics and felt needs.

2. Next, your group could break up into smaller groups, each small group choosing a particular subset for its reflection. It is important to develop a list of the most pressing needs of the unchurched people in each one of the subsets your group has identified. What are the people like who comprise these various groups? What are their

needs? And what shape in word and deed may the gospel take that is good news for them?

3. Now that the various needs have been identified in each subset, make a note regarding the way your congregation is or is not already responding to those needs. Consider every possible way that your church may meet some of those needs. At this point it is important for the group to identify some of the strengths of your congregation as it presently exists. What are the best things presently happening in your church? How can you focus these strengths both on the needs of the members of your church and on the needs of the various subsets of people that comprise your context? Affirm these strengths and build on them.

It may be that the needs of some of the unchurched in your church's context are so urgent, pressing, complex, and large that your church cannot adequately respond to them by itself. In that case, your church may need to create a network of several churches that *together* can respond to those needs. If this is done, issues of relational faith-sharing and incorporation into the church need to be intentionally brought up, clearly discussed, and carefully included in the planning. Especially in the city, we have had far too much "doing-for" people and far too little conversion, empowerment, and incorporation into the church of those who have been recipients of our ministries.

4. Such a needs-analysis must be complemented with a potentials-analysis. Very often evangelistic congregations do not need to do more. They just need to focus more intentionally on what they already are doing. In other words, sometimes the most fruitful place to begin is to reflect on the programs, people, and webs of relationships that are already in place, and to see them as potentials for relational evangelism. This calls for us to look at ourselves and our congregation from the perspective of the people of the various subsets in the church's context. It means we need to reexamine the various arenas of our church's life and programs, looking at their potential for relational evangelism among the various subgroups of unchurched people.

ACTION

Hopefully your evangelism task force will not end its discussion without translating some of what has been said into a commitment to concrete action.

1. There may be some major issues that surfaced in the above discussion that call for intentional, concerted prayer. Challenge each other to pray for at least one of the subsets of people you have identified, as well as for the various aspects of the life of your congregation that have been analyzed.

2. What new action steps do you feel need to be taken to maximize your congregation's potential to reach the nonchurched in the various subsets of the people of its context?

3. Usually the discussion suggested above will yield many things that need attention, change, and action. I challenge your group, through prayer and discussion, to set down the two or three new action steps that seem to a) have the highest potential for building relational evangelism, b) are based on some of the congregation's major strengths, and c) provide the most effective and natural steps toward focusing the life of your congregation outward.

4. Go and do what you have committed yourself to do, saturating your activity in prayer, trusting deeply in the power of the Holy Spirit, depending on God to guide you in the endeavor, and waiting on God to bring about the desired results.

[1] A highly respected sociologist of religion, Robert Wuthnow, emphasized the importance of this interaction between congregation and surrounding context in "Evangelicals, Liberals, and the Perils of Individualism," *Perspectives* (VI:5, May 1991), pp. 10-13. Wuthnow conducted a survey that sought to correlate individual faith, participation in a local congregation, and charitable activities in the community. His conclusion was that "In general, the more often an individual claims to experience divine love, the more likely that person is to spend time on charitable activities. But this effect is limited to individuals who attend church regularly. Among individuals who attend church infrequently or who do not attend, how much or how little they feel God's love has no effect on the likelihood of their being involved in charitable work" (p. 13).

[2] Harvie Conn, *Evangelism: Doing Justice and Preaching Grace* (Grand Rapids: Zondervan, 1982).

[3] See Charles Van Engen, "Can Older Churches Grow in the City?" *Global Church Growth* (XXVI: 1, January-March 1989), pp. 15-16; and Charles Van Engen, *God's Missionary People: Rethinking the Purpose of the Local Church* (Grand Rapids: Baker, 1991).

CHAPTER TEN

Mobilizing the Entire Congregation for Witness

(Acts 2.1-47)

In the last chapter we emphasized the corporate nature of the congregation as the people of God who are called to witness of their faith in a specific context. Our major focus was the way a congregation views the various subsets of people within its context—and how the church responds to them. In other words, we were looking outward with a corporate perspective, attempting to listen, understand, and present the gospel in terms that are relevant to the social structures of the church's surrounding context. In effect, we were repeating what we learned in Chapters Two, Three, and Four—except that we were seeing the process in relation to the larger sociological units, rather than focusing on particular individuals. We were analyzing the larger social subsets of people as a way of more effectively understanding, listening, and ministering to our neighbors.

There is one last step we need to take before we find ourselves coming back full circle to where we began in Chapter One. We now need to look inward again at our congregation. This time, rather than looking at the congregation as a sum of various individual witnesses, we need to look at it corporately, as a social unit that carries out its witness through a number of evangelistic programs.

EXPOSITION

Please read Acts 2.1-47 once more. I want you to read it this time not from the perspective of seeing individuals, but rather from the perspective of seeing the group as an organic whole. Acts 2 speaks of a body of believers who receive the Holy Spirit. This group speaks through the mouth of Peter, shapes its life in a particular way, impacts its social context, and experiences continued growth as "day by day the Lord added to their number those who were being saved" (2.47).

The corporate nature of the church receives stronger and stronger emphasis as one reads through the book of Acts. It isn't long before the Jerusalem house churches discover that the Holy Spirit has given rise to a group of believers in Samaria. Then they hear about a body of Christians in Antioch. Soon after, they are astounded by the stories that Paul and Barnabas and their companions return to tell concerning the numerous groups of believers that begin to dot the map of the Roman Empire.

Clearly the Holy Spirit is actively building something that is more than the sum of its parts—a corporate organism that seems to have a life of its own. Later Paul tries to explain this by saying that as the members of the organism participate in ministry (inside and outside the church), they build up the body of Christ "until all of us come to unity of the faith and of the knowledge of the Son of God, to growth, to the measure of the full stature of Christ" (Eph. 4.13). Peter tries to explain it by using the image of a building: "Come to him, a living stone...and like living stones, let yourselves be built into a spiritual house, to be a holy priesthood, to offer spiritual sacrifices acceptable to God through Jesus Christ" (1 Pet. 2.4-5).

As you witnessed to your neighbor during the course of this evangelism study, you were in fact participating in a corporate event that entailed the growth of the body of Christ. As your neighbor heard the gospel presented in an understandable and empathetic way, and as your neighbor responded in faith through the Holy Spirit's work, he or she was also taking part in a corporate event whereby the Holy Spirit was embracing that person as a living stone, to be added to the building which is the church.

When your neighbor formally becomes a member of your church through baptism and incorporation into the various aspects of the life of your church, that outward reception is really only a sign that points to a much deeper spiritual reality. The real issue is that your neighbor is one of the "living stones" (1 Pet. 2.5) whom God had chosen "before the foundation of the world" (Eph. 1.4) to be added to the family of God, the church. As Luke says, "the Lord added to their number those who were being saved" (Acts 2.47; underline mine). In the final analysis you and I do not choose those whom we want to have as part of the church. Rather, Jesus Christ calls those whom he wishes to invite through the work of the Holy Spirit—and they are the ones added to our number.

This does not minimize our role in the growth of God's kingdom. Luke in no way wants to downplay the responsibility of Christians to witness concerning their faith. God does use human instruments—and they are the members of the body of Christ. God seldom works apart from human agency. Christian witness is crucial and essential. It is an integral part of the process through which the Spirit gathers those who are to be added to the church. Philip, for example, is sent to meet the Ethiopian. And even though the Holy Spirit has prepared the heart and mind of the Ethiopian as he reads Isaiah, Philip's part is crucial in explaining to the Ethiopian the essentials of faith in Jesus Christ and incorporating him into the church through baptism (see Acts 8.26-40).

Without Luke's strong emphasis on human agency in Christian witness, the rest of the book of Acts, and especially Paul's journeys, would be unnecessary and make little sense. Although God through Jesus Christ by the work of the Holy Spirit is the one who convicts, calls, redeems, converts, gathers, and incorporates our neighbor, still God has chosen to do that primarily through our witness. "You will be my witnesses" is not an added feature to the story; it is the heart of the story.

REFLECTION

You and your converted neighbor are now part of a larger corporate whole, the body of Christ. The very meaning and significance of your being Christians is tied up in your belonging to the household of God, the corporate body of witnesses.

One of the most important aspects of this corporate perspective of the witnessing community involves a careful look at the way evangelism is built into the life and programs of your congregation. If at its heart the church is to be Christ's witness, then the most important agenda of its life and activities must be to witness to the unchurched regarding the gospel of Jesus Christ. Here we are asking something more basic than whether your congregation happens to have an evangelism "program." And we are asking for something more intentional than saying that everything the church does is aimed at witnessing.

Remember that at the beginning of this study we noted that the effective witness is the one who communicates the gospel in response to the concerns, perspectives, commitments, and agendas of the hearer, our neighbor. So a congregation's evangelistic activities are to be judged on the basis of whether unchurched neighbors are in fact being impacted by the corporate witness of your congregation. In relation to all that we have studied so far, the implications of this corporate perspective may be presented as follows:

1. The neighbor's felt needs and social context are the KEYS to effective corporate witness.

2. The Holy Spirit is the POWER AND PRESENCE of the church's corporate witness.

3. The witnessing Christian is the INSTRUMENT through which the Holy Spirit points to Jesus Christ.

4. The church is the STRUCTURE AND ENVIRONMENT in which corporate witness takes place.

5. The social context in a particular time and place is the ARENA of the church's corporate witness.

Based on the centrality of the neighbor in the entire process of corporate witness, you may be able to suggest ways in which your evangelism task force could judge your church's over-all involvement in relational evangelism. Here are some of the issues that need to be examined:

1. The involvement, commitment, and climate of your church for neighbor-oriented relational evangelism.

2. The extent to which the members of your congregation are prepared to be neighbor-oriented and to listen carefully to those who are not yet in the church.

3. The degree to which your church commits itself to pray for the neighbors that comprise your church's various contextual "communities."

4. The way your church tends to communicate its message. Does it seek to present the gospel in a way that is appropriate to the neighbors in its context?

5. The extent that your congregation actually communicates the message. Does the communication in fact reach those for whom it has been prepared?

6. The way your neighbor interprets the message which your church seeks to communicate.

7. The willingness of your congregation to incorporate your neighbor.

8. How your neighbor was taught and modeled with regard to Christian fellowship and Christian outreach and ministry in the surrounding context.

9. The extent to which your congregation equipped your converted neighbor for ministry in society as part of your church's outreach.

10. The degree to which the leaders and programs of your church are evaluated on the basis of what is being done in witness in the world.

Far too often we tend to evaluate our pastoral staff, leadership, and programming on the basis of what happens inside the church for the benefit of the members. An evangelizing congregation will evaluate its leaders and programs on a completely different basis. For an evangelizing church the bottom line is the impact that the leaders and programs have on those who are yet not part of the church. What programs are able to attract, enfold, gather and incorporate new converts? And what programs are able to equip, direct, send forth, and encourage the church's members for witness in the surrounding context? The leaders of the church have a responsibility to see that the church as a corporate organism is simultaneously gathering and sending the members as witnesses of Jesus Christ in the "communities" of the church.

And so we have come full circle. We are again anticipating the coming of the Spirit, to descend on us in a new Pentecost and to propel us outward beyond the boundaries of our congregation—out into the streets, the businesses, the neighborhoods, the schools, the homes of the context in which God has placed us. Again we prepare ourselves to carefully listen to our neighbors, to sensitively craft our message, to earnestly pray for the Spirit's work of conversion, to lovingly incorporate the new converts, and to be amazed all over again at God's grace in continuing to add to our number those who are being saved.

As we saw in Chapter One, there are some very clear obstacles to our witness in the North American setting. Very little sense of a need for God, a weak understanding of the public dimensions of faith, and a deformed understanding of conversion make it difficult for many North Americans to hear the gospel. We also saw that there are barriers inside our churches. Lack of clarity about what constitutes evangelism, as well as a basic lack of understanding concerning the essentials of the faith, tend to muffle our witness.

Hopefully, through this study we have discovered the amazing opportunities open to us for natural, unforced, sensitive, honest, and caring witness to our neighbors. Hopefully we have learned that our witness is greatly facilitated when we learn to allow the Holy Spirit to make us very intentional about our relationships, our prayers, our listening, and our speaking with those who as yet do not know Jesus Christ. Hopefully we have begun to catch a glimpse of how God sees our lives as we constantly move back and forth between Christian and non-Christian contexts. Hopefully we have gained a new vision for the way our congregations can become active organisms whose entire life is focused on those who have not yet heard—and on facilitating its members to more intentionally and effectively share the gospel in word and deed with those who are not yet Christian.

DISCUSSION

Go back to the ten issues mentioned above. The facilitator of your evangelism task force may want to plan on at least a half hour in which the members of the group reflect together concerning these issues. How would your group go about helping your congregation create new opportunities for natural relational witness with the persons you chose as your neighbors for this course of study? Give some thought to the strengths and weaknesses of your church's congregational life when viewed from the perspective of your neighbor. Then brainstorm how your church might be helped to maximize its potential for relational evangelism.

ACTION

1. After some sharing of viewpoints, your group may want to suggest some evangelistic activities that would be important for your church to do in the near future.
2. Commit yourself to finding specific ways in which your congregation can facilitate your converted neighbors to become active witnesses in their own right, evangelizing their neighbors the same way they were evangelized.
3. Decide who in your evangelism group will approach various people and structures in your church to bring about the necessary changes you envision.

Toward the end of this last evening, it would probably be helpful and inspirational for the group to spend some time reflecting together on their experiences during the past ten weeks. What surprises were there? What feelings and ideas about evangelism were confirmed? What new ideas were learned? What individuals were converted during this time, and how did it happen? What new actions were taken by members of the group? What plans do the members have for continuing their commitment to relational witness to their neighbor?

Now spend at least a half hour in prayer together. Pray for each witness, that what has been learned these ten weeks will become a lifestyle of relational witness for many years to come. Pray for each neighbor to whom the members of the group have sought to witness. Pray for those neighbors who have been converted during these ten weeks. Especially pray for their incorporation into the church and for their own witness to a new set of neighbors. Give thanks and praise to God for each other, for the ten weeks of learning and pilgrimage in relational evangelism. Pray for each other, that each member of the group will continue to discover new ways in which their faith-journey may be tapped as a resource for intentional, natural, appropriate, and sensitive witness to the presence of Jesus Christ in your lives.

Appendix A

A Parable of Fishless Fishermen

John M. Dresscher

Issue: Is a person a fisherman if year after year he never catches any fish?

Now it came to pass that a group existed who called themselves fishermen. And lo, there were many fish in the waters all around. In fact the whole area was surrounded by streams and lakes filled with fish. And the fish were hungry.

Week after week, month after month, and year after year these who called themselves fishermen met in meetings and talked about their call to fish, the abundance of fish, and how they might go about fishing. Year after year they carefully defined what fishing means, defended fishing as an occupation, and declared that fishing is always to be a primary task of fishermen.

Continually they searched for new and better methods of fishing and for new and better definitions of fishing. Further they said, "The fishing industry exists by fishing as fire exists by burning." They loved slogans such as "Fishing is the task of every fisherman," "Every fisherman is a fisher," and "A fisherman's outpost for every fisherman's club." They sponsored special meetings called

---

— Mennonite pastor John M. Drescher is the author of *Testimony of Triumph*, *Meditations for the Newly Married*, *What Should Parents Expect?*, and other books.

This article appeared first in *Church Growth: America* magazine, September-October 1978. Used by permission.

"Fishermen's Campaigns" and "The Month for Fishermen to Fish." They sponsored costly nationwide and worldwide congresses to discuss fishing and to promote fishing and hear about all the ways of fishing such as the new fishing equipment, fish calls, and whether any new bait was discovered.

These fishermen built large, beautiful buildings called "Fishing Headquarters." The plea was that everyone should be a fisherman and every fisherman should fish. One thing they didn't do, however; they didn't fish.

In addition to meeting regularly, they organized a board to send out fishermen to other places where there were many fish. All the fishermen seemed to agree that what is needed is a board which could challenge fishermen to be faithful in fishing. The board was formed by those who had the great vision and courage to speak about fishing, to define fishing, and to promote the idea of fishing in faraway streams and lakes where many other fish of different colors lived.

Also the board hired staffs and appointed committees and held many meetings to define fishing, to defend fishing, and to decide what new streams should be thought about. But the staff and committee members did not fish.

Large, elaborate, and expensive training centers were built whose original and primary purpose was to teach fishermen how to fish. Over the years courses were offered on the needs of fish, the nature of fish, where to find fish, the psychological reactions of fish, and how to approach and feed fish. Those who taught had doctorates in fishology. But the teachers did not fish. They only taught fishing. Year after year, after tedious training, many were graduated and were given fishing licenses. They were sent to do full-time fishing, some to distant waters which were filled with fish.

Some spent much study and travel to learn the history of fishing and to see faraway places where the founding fathers did great fishing in the centuries past. They lauded the faithful fishermen of years before who handed down the idea of fishing.

Further, the fishermen built large printing houses to publish fishing guides. Presses were kept busy day and night to produce materials solely devoted to fishing methods, equipment, and programs to arrange and to encourage meetings to talk about fishing. A speakers' bureau was also provided to schedule special speakers on the subject of fishing.

Many who felt the call to be fishermen responded. They were commissioned and sent to fish. But like the fishermen back home they never fished. Like the fishermen back home they engaged in all kinds of other occupations. They built power plants to pump water for fish and tractors to plow new waterways. They made all kinds of equipment to travel here and there to look at fish hatcheries.

Some also said they wanted to be part of the fishing party, but they felt called to furnish fishing equipment. Others felt their job was to relate to the fish in a good way so the fish would know the difference between good and bad fishermen. Others felt that simply letting the fish know they were nice, land-loving neighbors and how loving and kind they were was enough.

After one stirring meeting on "The Necessity for Fishing," one young fellow left the meeting and went fishing. The next day he reported he had caught two outstanding fish. He was honored for his excellent catch and scheduled to visit all the big meetings possible to tell how he did it. So he quit his fishing in order to have time to tell about the experience to the other fishermen. He was also placed on the Fishermen's General Board as a person having considerable experience.

Now it's true that many of the fishermen sacrificed and put up with all kinds of difficulties. Some lived near the water and bore the smell of dead fish every day. They received the ridicule of some who made fun of their fishermen's clubs and the fact that they claimed to be fishermen yet never fished. They wondered about those who felt it was of little use to attend the weekly meetings to talk about fishing. After all, were they not following the Master who said, "Follow me, and I will make you fishers of men"?

Imagine how hurt some were when one day a person suggested that those who didn't catch fish were really not fishermen, no matter how much they claimed to be. Yet it did sound correct. Is a person a fisherman if year after year he never catches a fish? Is one following if he isn't fishing?

Appendix B

Evangelism in Reformed Perspective: An Evangelism Manifesto

As Christians in the Reformed tradition, holding to the Scriptures as the Word of God, we joyfully confess our faith in Jesus Christ as Savior and Lord and our unity with all Christians in the world mission of his church. We share the newly-expressed concern of believers everywhere to understand the nature of evangelism and its place in our total task. We deplore our own tendencies in thought and action to separate gospel proclamation from compassionate ministry. We believe that both are rightly understood only in the light of the Bible's pervasive theme—the kingdom of God.

The Proclamation of the Kingdom

We affirm that to *evangelize* is to proclaim the good news of God's reign. The sense of *public proclamation* is always dominant in the biblical use of the term. Evangelists are "bringers of the gospel." The

---

direct object of the verb "to evangelize" is rarely the hearers or recipients of the message. That is, the apostles are not usually said to "evangelize" *people*. They "evangelize" a word, a content, *to* people (Acts 8.4; 15.35; Rom. 1.15). *What* they "evangelize" is variously described as "the gospel" (Rom. 1.15), "the Word of the Lord" (1 Peter 1.25), "the faith" (Rom. 10.8; Gal. 1.23), "Jesus" (Acts 5.42, 17.18), "Christ" (Phil. 1.8), or, comprehensively, "the kingdom of God" (Acts 8.12, 20.25, 28.23,31).

The proclamation is "good news" (1 Peter 1.25). The note of gladness is an essential part of it. To evangelize is to bring "good tidings of great joy" (Isa. 52.7, 8; Luke 2.10) at which believing hearers "break forth into singing" (Isa. 54.1, 55.12; Acts 2.41-46, 8.5-8, 35, 39, 16.30-34). The "kingdom of God is like a treasure . . ." (Matt. 13.44).

In both Testaments to "evangelize" is to proclaim a victory, to *herald a new reign* (Isa. 61.1; Luke 4.18, 19). At heart it is to testify that "the kingdom of God has drawn near!" (Matt. 4.17, 10.7; Mark 1.14-15).

This "kingdom," in biblical usage, refers not primarily to the divine sovereignty in a general sense, but to the active, saving reign of the Triune God in history. The coming kingdom is not static but dynamic, not so much a concept as a ruling power. To proclaim "the kingdom of God has drawn near" is to herald those mighty events in which God's royal rule has invaded the earth in the coming of Jesus Christ and in the power of the Holy Spirit. It is to bring the thrilling news of God's victory in the death and resurrection of his Son over all the powers of darkness that have enslaved mankind and made his good creation subject to bondage (Col. 1.13-14; Rom. 8.19-25). It is to tell of what God has done to bring forgiveness to the guilty, help to the poor, release to the captives, sight to the blind, deliverance to the oppressed. It is to announce to the whole creation a divine reign of justice and peace (Luke 2.14; Acts 10.36; Eph. 2.17).

Together with this grand announcement, the proclamation of the kingdom brings a summons. Hearers are called to renounce all sin, each false lord, every rival sovereignty, and to submit through repentance and faith to God's saving reign in Christ (Mark 6.12; Acts 17.30, 26.20). The proclamation demands commitment to God's lordship and obedience to his will in the world (Matt. 7.21). Although the decisive victory over the forces of evil has been won, the conflict still rages (Eph. 6.11, 12). Christ is risen; the Spirit has been poured out upon the church; the powers of the coming age are at work in the world, but the end is not yet. Hosts of darkness resist God's sovereignty; rampant evils oppose his will. To repent and believe is to side with God's purpose in this conflict—assured of ultimate victory, while contending God's righteousness in every sphere of life (1 Cor. 15.54-57; Acts 26.16-18).

We affirm, accordingly, that all evangelizing in the New Testament sense of the term includes the joyous proclamation of God's saving rule, together with the call to repent and believe the gospel (Acts 20.21).

The Signs of the Kingdom

The proclamation of God's kingly rule brings with it the reality proclaimed. "Evangelizing" is never seen in the New Testament as a merely human activity or as a word which stands alone. "The kingdom of God does not consist in talk, but in power" (1 Cor. 4.20). The gospel of the kingdom comes "not only in word, but also in power, and in the Holy Spirit, and with full conviction" (1 Thess. 1.5). In our Lord's ministry, evangelizing always occurs in connection with other signs that the kingdom has drawn near. "Preaching good news to the poor," for example, is closely linked with "setting at liberty those who are oppressed." As evidence that the kingdom of God has come in his ministry, Jesus gives the following: "the blind receive their sight and the lame walk, lepers are cleansed and the deaf hear, the dead are raised up and the poor have good news preached to them" (Matt. 11.5; Luke 4.18, 19). The acts of healing and restoration are clearly distinguished from "evangelizing," yet they are not isolated from it. In like manner the life of the church itself, as a loving, serving community, bears witness to the proclaimed kingdom. Her works of mercy and power are among the signs of its presence (Acts 1.8).

We affirm, then, that all evangelizing in the New Testament sense of the term is accompanied by the signs of God's kingdom among his people and springs from their active concern for the full deliverance and restoration of all to whom the gospel is addressed. Only in this way is the church's message an authentic heralding of God's saving rule. The caring ministry of the Christian fellowship and her redemptive action in the world form the indispensable context for faithful proclamation. We must show ourselves "ready to share not only the gospel of God but also ourselves . . ." (1 Thess. 2.8).

The Imperative of the Kingdom

Christ sends his church to make disciples of all nations (Matt. 28.19, 20). The gospel of the kingdom brings the only hope of salvation for lost mankind (Acts 4.12). All stand under the judgment of which it warns; all need the forgiveness and new life it offers; all are summoned to the commitment it demands (John 3.16-21).

The same good news preached to the world must be constantly heard afresh in the church, for the call to repent and believe, to submit to God's gracious reign, is a call to growth as well as to conversion. The church lives by the gospel it proclaims (2 Cor. 5.15).

The Spirit calls God's people to live in genuine community (1 John 1.3-4) and to pursue love and justice in the world (1 John 3.16-18; 1 Tim. 6.17-19; Titus 2.11-14). Thus the church by its life and work points to the ruling power of the risen Lord.

We affirm, therefore, our responsibility to proclaim, to manifest and to serve the kingdom of God. We confess our dependence on the Holy Spirit for power to fulfill our calling until Christ comes to glory. In gratitude for the grace given us, and in confidence that our labor is not in vain, we commit ourselves anew to this mission, praying as we go, "Thy kingdom come!" (Matt. 6.10).

Evangelism and the Kingdom of God

God's Reign

How are we to understand *evangelism*? The term is familiar enough, but there is by no means a consensus among Christians as to what it means. Traditionally, evangelism has been defined as "preaching the gospel" or "the winning of personal commitments to Christ." Today, however, many prefer to give it a much wider meaning. For them, evangelism is "everything the church does" and its goal can be described as the "humanizing" or "liberation" of all people. Some argue that evangelism must always be verbal, while others contend that it finds most significant expression in deeds or personal presence. While many see it as the province of spiritually gifted persons, more and more of us are coming to look upon evangelism as a calling for all Christians. What precisely is it to "evangelize," and what kind of theology should underlie our practice of it?

It was to deal with questions like these that the Reformed Church in America and the Christian Reformed Church appointed in 1973 a joint committee to "study the theology of evangelism." Our committee found this to be a large, challenging, exciting task. We considered a number of alternatives in seeking to fulfill it. Should we add a few volumes of our own to an already vast literature on the subject? Should we attempt to evaluate existing programs in evangelism from the standpoint of the Scriptures and the Reformed faith? Should we seek to encourage our respective churches in some form of united witness?

One specific goal impressed us as primary. We wanted to state, in relatively brief compass, our common convictions about the work of evangelism. We were especially concerned to set forth the relationship between gospel proclamation and other forms of ministry to human need. Too often, we felt, evangelism and social concern had been either confusedly identified with one another or else set at opposite poles, each with its own defenders. And even when both were insisted on as crucially important (as in documents like the Lausanne Covenant) they were often seen as merely parallel activities without vital connection to each other. In the course of our study, however, we became more and more convinced that "both are rightly understood only in the light of the Bible's pervasive theme—the kingdom of God."

That quotation is from a document entitled, "An Evangelism Manifesto." A manifesto, as you may recall, is a "public declaration of intentions, motives or views." The joint committee has prepared this particular declaration for study and evaluation by our respective churches. We have received from various individuals, consistories and agencies, a good deal of helpful response and inquiry. We hope in this and in subsequent articles to develop more fully the view expressed in the Manifesto, and to highlight certain of its implications.

Do the Scriptures of the Old and New Testaments, in spite of all their rich diversity, present a single theme? Can we find one dominant motif, from Genesis to Revelation, from creation to consummation? Christians have always answered in the affirmative.

Some maintain that Jesus Christ is the central message of the Scriptures, and there is much to support that claim. Every book of the New Testament is written from the standpoint of faith in the risen Christ. And as for the Old Testament, did not Jesus expound to his disciples "in all the scriptures the things concerning himself"?

Our Lord surely saw the Scriptures, from beginning to end, as bearing witness to him. But in all his teaching, he consistently viewed that witness in a wider context. The Son had come, in the power of the Holy Spirit, to do the will of the Father. Jesus was Messiah, Savior, and Lord by God's appointment. In all he said about himself, his master theme was "the kingdom of God."

Matthew and Mark both summarize the preaching of Jesus in words like these: "Now after that John was arrested, Jesus came into Galilee, preaching the gospel of God, and saying 'The time is fulfilled, and the kingdom of God is at hand'" (Mark 1.14-15). Luke records Jesus as declaring, "I must preach the kingdom of God" (Luke 4.43). And although the phrase is not used as frequently in the fourth Gospel, it is still obviously central. When Jesus talks with Nicodemus about the mysteries of the new birth, he is telling him what is required to "see" and "enter" the kingdom of God (John 3.3, 5).

Turn to the Sermon on the Mount to see how the kingdom of God theme dominates Jesus' teaching. Everything is referred to "the kingdom of God" or its equivalent, "the kingdom of heaven." Our Lord's opening words are, "Blessed are the poor in spirit; for theirs is the kingdom of heaven!" (Matt. 5.3). He goes on to speak of "entering the kingdom," being "called great" in it, praying for its coming, and seeking it as our number one priority in life.

Read Jesus' parables and the same cumulative effect is overwhelming: almost every one develops in some way "what the kingdom of God is like." Note Matthew 13, for example. These are the "mysteries" of the kingdom of heaven. They deal with the "word" of the Kingdom, with its growth, its preciousness, its awesome final judgement. To understand what Jesus taught was to be in his words "a scribe who has been trained for the kingdom of heaven" (Matt. 13.52).

What about the rest of the New Testament? The Book of Acts begins by describing how for 40 days the risen Jesus spoke to his disciples "speaking of the kingdom of God" (Acts 1.3). The book ends with Paul at Rome, receiving people into his own hired house, and "preaching the kingdom of God" (Acts 28.30-31).

In Paul's writings, the term itself is not a common one, but the reality behind it is on every page. This apostle's equivalent for "the kingdom of God" is the phrase *kurios Iesous*—"Jesus is Lord." In Jesus, that is, God's kingdom has come among us.

And what about the book of the Revelation? The royal note is sounded there again and again until finally "the kingdom of the world has become the kingdom of our Lord and of his Christ, and he shall reign forever and ever" (Rev. 11.15). "Hallelujah, for the Lord God the Almighty reigns!" (Rev. 19.6).

Those last words give us the key to an understanding of this biblical phrase, "the kingdom of God." It expresses *God's active reign*. We use the word "kingdom" at times to refer to a territory or a group over which a king rules. Kingship may imply also a status or quality in the king. But the biblical theme is dynamic, not static. It describes not titles or territories, but the exercise of ruling *power*. Jesus says to the Pharisees, for example, "If it is by the Spirit of God that I cast our demons, then the kingdom of God has come upon you" (Matt. 12.28). These mighty deliverances, in other words, are the signs of a new divine reign. God's kingdom comes with conquering strength.

But in what sense does it *"come"* or *"draw near"*? How can we speak of it as something *new*? Hasn't God always ruled? Isn't he, from the beginning, the sovereign Lord of the universe? Yes, most certainly. But the rebellion of his creatures has brought about an altered situation in this world. By their own willful revolt, men and women have come under the rule of sin, under the dominion of Satan and the powers of darkness. Having defied their rightful king, they live under the tyranny and enslavement of another.

The Old Testament points to, prepares for, and promises what God will do about this situation. The tiptoe anticipation of the prophets is toward the coming reign of God. Listen to these words of joyous expectation:

Say among the nations, "The Lord reigns!"
Let the heavens be glad, and let the earth rejoice;
let the sea roar, and all that fills it;
let the field exult, and everything in it!
Then shall the trees of the wood
Sing for joy before the Lord, for he comes,
for he comes to judge the earth!
He will judge the world with righteousness
and the peoples with his truth.
(Ps. 96.10a, 11-13)

And recall this prayer of longing for a righteous redeemer-king:

May he judge thy people with righteousness
and thy poor with justice!
May he defend the cause of the poor of the people,
give deliverance to the needy and crush the oppressor!
May all kings fall down before him,
all nations serve him!
(Ps. 72.2, 4, 11)

What the Old Testament prays for, longs, for, hopes for, the New Testament announces, "The King has come! The kingdom has drawn near." God has come in person to establish his reign. That is the thrill and throb of gospel proclamation. Here is our world groaning under alien rule, duped by the false gods we have followed. Suddenly he comes, the Lord against whom we have rebelled, the one born to be King. He comes in Jesus Christ to save and to rule! "Lift up your heads, O gates! Lift them up, you everlasting doors, and the King of glory shall come in!"

Questions on "God's Reign"

1. What has been your understanding of the term "evangelism"?
2. How have you understood the relationship between gospel proclamation and other forms of ministry to human need?
3. Express in one sentence what you believe to be the central message of the Bible.
4. What ideas come to your mind when you hear the phrase, "the kingdom of God"?
5. In what sense has God's kingdom already come, and in what sense is it still to come?

Proclaim the Good News

Do you remember when our astronauts returned after the first moon landing? There had been tense moments during their space Odyssey. Malfunctioning equipment at several points had threatened the success of their mission and placed their lives in jeopardy. But all these difficulties had been overcome; their visit to the moon had electrified the world. Now they were almost back home, and were encountering the fearful pressures and temperatures of "re-entry." For a few agonizing minutes radio contact was lost. All eyes from the waiting U.S. fleet were fixed on the heavens. Suddenly the first bright chute flashed into view. A cheer went up on every deck. Millions beamed, wept for joy, and gave thanks to God as they heard the news by television and radio. The brave men of space were back—safe at last!

If we can relive those moments, we can feel perhaps something of the joy of ancient Jerusalem when the exiles returned from Babylon. For them, the anxious waiting was not for days and weeks, but for years and weary decades. God's people had been carried away in shame and suffering to a distant land. A few survivors had been left in the holy city to mourn the glories of the past and cherish a flickering hope for the future. Would the ransomed of the Lord ever return?

Then a marvelous thing had happened. The conquering Cyrus, God's unwitting servant, had decreed that Babylon's long-held captives should go free. Fleet messengers had carried the news far and wide: the exiles were on their way home. Now all Jerusalem was standing on the walls and towers, sons perched on their fathers' shoulders, craning for a glimpse of that returning company. There, on the crest of a hill, appeared a forerunner, a herald. "Ho, friend, what's the word?" Then came the thrilling answer, "Your God reigns!" (Isa. 52.7).

What a moment! Trampled dreams up on their feet again, longing eyes drinking in the sight of a storied city, a battered faith vindicated at last! Here were poor, chastened people toiling up the slopes to Jerusalem. But the watchers on the walls were called to see in their coming a vision supremely grand: "Behold, your God!" (Isa. 40.9). "This is the Lord's doing and it is marvelous in our eyes!"

It is that scene which is celebrated in the Old Testament's greatest word about evangelism: "How beautiful upon the mountains are the feet of him who brings good tidings, who publishes salvation, who says to Zion, 'Your God reigns' " (Isa. 52.7). The apostle Paul quotes this passage when he describes the work of those who preach the gospel (Rom. 10.15). Our Lord himself announces his ministry of proclaiming "good news to the poor" by citing related passages (Isa. 61.1-2; Luke 4.17-18). All that the New Testament says about evangelizing harks back to, and draws inspiration from, prophetic words like these. What can we find here today that will illumine our understanding of evangelism?

Surely this: *to evangelize is to proclaim a message*. An act of announcement, of heralding, is always in view. The prophet sings of one who "brings tidings," who "publishes," who "speaks to Zion" a momentous word. The verbs "to evangelize" and "to preach" are used almost synonymously in the New Testament. Both envisage a declaration of events—something like the "Hear ye! Hear ye!" of a town crier. Evangelizing has the thrust of a special bulletin that interrupts ordinary television programming, or a six-inch newspaper headline.

The act of proclamation is so central to the term that it would be needless to labor the point were it not for the blurred usage to which "evangelism" has been subjected in our time. But whatever else may be accomplished by "silence," by "witness without speaking the Name," by the ministry of personal presence," or by various forms of "Christian action," none of these fulfills the task of "evangelizing." All are closely related to it (as we shall show in subsequent articles) but none can possibly take its place. "Evangelism," as someone has put it, "is the meeting of a life with a life—plus a *word*"—the word of the gospel.

That points up our second affirmation: *to evangelize is to proclaim good news*. In both its Hebrew and Greek roots, the idea of a *joyful* message is an essential part of the verb. In the ancient world, the happy news could be the birth of a child, the homecoming of a loved one, a deliverance from distress or a signal victory in battle. It's the kind of thing you would shout across the street to the neighbors you know best: "The promotion came through!" "The operation was a success!" "John's come home!" or maybe, "Have you heard? The war's over!"

When people receive the evangel, rejoicing always follows. As those messengers with "beautiful feet" arrive in Jerusalem, the "watchmen lift up their voice, together they sing for joy" (Isa. 52.8). When Philip "evangelized the word" to the people of Samaria, "there was much joy in that city" (Acts 8.4, 8).

It is well to remind ourselves that evangelists are joy-bringers. Not everything we Christians say to the world is "evangelism." A dear lady once told me with great excitement that she had just "witnessed" to her neighbor. When I inquired about it, she reported that she had seen the man next door washing his car on Sunday. Her witness consisted in telling him that "he shouldn't do that." She may have been giving good advice, but she hardly communicated good news!

A question to ponder: have we succeeded in communicating to people around us, or even to those within our membership, that the Christian church has great glad tidings to tell? What about the young people who grow up in our homes and congregations? Would they describe the basic message they have heard from us as a piece of thrillingly good news?

Finally, the gospel which the first Christians preached was *the good news of God's reign*. The beginning of a new regime has always been a time of joy and expectation. In the Greco-Roman world to "evangelize" often meant to announce the accession of a new monarch. This was a call to hope and celebration. And today, aren't Americans of every political persuasion moved by inaugural ceremonies as they hope for a better future?

Think again of the heralds who brought glad tidings to Jerusalem. They told of what God had done for his people in redeeming them from bondage and returning them to their beloved home. For those messengers, this divine deliverance taught one luminous truth: "Your God *reigns*." Here is fresh evidence of his saving rule!

All of this lies in the background of New Testament evangelizing. Here also it is a matter of proclaiming events—the mighty acts of God in Christ. Jesus went about doing good, and healing all who were oppressed by the devil. He was crucified and raised from the dead on the third day. He appeared to chosen witnesses. God has highly exalted him, and poured out through him the Holy Spirit. This Jesus will come again to judge the living and the dead!

But these events are the "gospel," the message of great good news, because of what they *mean*—their divinely given significance. Christ died *for our sins*, heralds the apostle Paul. "He was raised *for our justification*." He ever lives *to intercede for us*. He comes in glory to receive us to himself. In Christ, God acts for us and for our salvation.

But too many of us stop there. We fail to see that the Bible's gospel is the gospel of the *kingdom*. The good news of God's *reign*. God has come in Jesus Christ to dethrone the false lords and conquer the evil powers that have held us in bondage. Our freedom, joy, and salvation lie only in submission to his rule.

We often act as though our personal solace, security, and success were ultimate goals. We can even preach these to others as "the good news." In themselves, they are not. That one-sided "gospel" may well confirm us in our self-centeredness. Had we eyes to see, ears to hear, we would know that the world's hope and our true good are bound up in this alone, that *Jesus Christ is Lord*, and that we are not our own but belong, body and soul, in life and death, joy and sorrow, success and failure, calm and storm, completely to him. "Hallelujah, for the Lord God the Almighty reigns!"

Questions on "Proclaim the Good News"

1. If "evangelizing" in the Bible clearly means proclaiming a message, how do you understand the effort of some to give it a much wider meaning?

2. Would you describe every part of the Bible's message as "good

news"? Explain your answer.

3. Why do you suppose that many people do not think of the Christian faith as "good tidings of great joy"?

4. What is the difference between a moral lesson and a gospel announcement?

5. In what sense is the proclamation "Jesus is Lord" a message of comfort and hope?

The Proclamation Brings a Summons!

To evangelize is to proclaim that God's redemptive rule has clearly come in Jesus Christ and in the power of his Spirit. The proclamation of the coming of that reign must confront men as an urgent call and summons. "God reigns in Christ. Therefore, repent and believe!" Sinful men may not stay as they are. Those who bring the glad news must urge men everywhere to repent and ally themselves with God.

Imagery taken from the Allied invasion of Europe in the Second World War will help clarify the nature of this urgent call to "repentance to God" and "faith in our Lord Jesus Christ" (Acts 20.21). As the Allies advanced through Europe after D-Day in 1943, subjugated peoples threw off Hitler's yoke and joined in routing their former captors. News of the coming liberation forces awakened hope and inspired courage in the occupied lands. As the allied armies swept eastward, radio broadcasts called on the people to defy Nazi orders and side openly with their liberators.

The gospel is the great news of God's action to free his enslaved world. Unlike most of the people in occupied countries during World War II, a sinful mankind has sided with its oppressor. We have not only been enslaved by the usurper Satan, but we have also been taken in by his deception and have joined the rebellion. But in the death and resurrection of his son, God has freed men from his just judgment against sin and has decisively defeated the alien power which held his good creation captive.

As the shock troops of the divine army of liberation sweep through the occupied territory, they announce the good news that deliverance has come. At the center of this marvelous proclamation is the truth that the Liberator has taken upon himself the judgement due his rebellious and traitorous subjects. When he came in person to establish a beachhead, they seized and killed him. Yet his death brought them life. Unlike any other battle casualty, the Lord Christ has passed through death and has returned to life. By satisfying the just claims of the Supreme Ruler against his wayward subjects, he has broken the power of the Enemy to dominate them. It is as if the rebels themselves had paid the penalty for their rebellion. With Paul they can exclaim, "I have been crucified with Christ; it is no longer

I who live, but Christ who lives in me!" (Gal. 2.20).

All who had joined forces with the occupying Enemy are called to stop aiding and abetting his cause and to change sides (Acts 2.38; 3.19; 17.30, 31). A reversal like that is painful as well as joyful. As their rightful Lord comes near in his power and love, their only proper response is to admit openly their sin of rebellion (1 John 1.10, 11), to express sorrow for it (2 Cor. 7.10), and publicly to pledge unswerving loyalty to the Liberator (Rom. 10.9, 10) even though the rear guard of the Enemy desperately tries to keep them in line (Phil. 1.28, 29). All who refuse to ally themselves with the new order can expect nothing but condemnation when the Conqueror comes in triumph to establish his rule completely (1 Thess. 1.10).

Clearly, repentance and conversion call for personal confession of sin, sorrow for sin and turning from it with joyful faith in Christ as Savior. But this saving faith must be seen in the larger context of the gospel of the kingdom. God is out to deliver, not only individuals here and there but a "corporation," a race and world lost in sin and alienated from him. In that campaign he calls his converts to become combatants for freedom and righteousness. Longing to be holy as he is holy and to see his righteous rule take hold everywhere, they contend for obedience to God in all relationships between persons and in every structure of society.

To repent and believe is to side with God and to receive his Holy Spirit for power to live and confess this new allegiance. It is to become more and more subject to the will of the Deliverer as that will calls us to obedience through the Scriptures. The dark powers which still try to regain lost territory can be turned back only by the sword of the Word wielded in the power of the Spirit.

To side with God in the fight, therefore, requires constant growth in knowing and doing the word of the Redeemer King. That word gives to the liberated a faithful record of the decisive battles in the war. It further challenges them to serve the new order in their times and circumstances, even at the cost of life itself.

To be the agents of God's new order through the wise and loving use of their abilities, the new allies must band together. The troops on still-occupied territory are called the "assembly," or the "church." They gather to praise their Lord and rededicate themselves to his cause. They relate to each other as the Liberator has related to them—in faithfulness and self-sacrificing love. They demonstrate what the liberated life looks like and feels like. This advance corps of the kingdom is the model of that new order of peace with God and man which is to come. Despite its imperfect obedience, infiltration by spies and betrayal by the unfaithful, the church bears the shape of the coming glory. She is the company of those who have repented, who now side with God in the conflict and who serve that realm in which righteousness, peace and joy in the Holy Spirit abound (Rom.

14.17). They have obeyed the gracious summons of the King.

Yet, those who have obeyed and who know the blessings of the kingdom have a restless sense of urgency for the salvation of others. They know that announcing the reign of God and exhibiting its effects in a preliminary way are not enough; proclamation must always be accompanied by the summons to all men to break with sin and side with God. Christ's command to bring the good news includes the command to call men to repentance and faith. Paul tells King Agrippa that Jesus commanded him to go to the Gentiles "to open their eyes, that they may turn from darkness to light and from the power of Satan to God" (Acts 26.18). Then Paul says that he obeyed the order and preached to the Gentiles "that they should repent and turn to God and perform deeds worthy of their repentance" (Acts 26.20). The company of the saved must follow the example of this great herald and apostle to the Gentiles, and in its practice it must demonstrate that New Testament evangelizing "includes the joyous proclamation of God's saving rule, together with the call to repent and believe the gospel."

Questions on "The Proclamation Brings a Summons"

1. If we understand the good news as God's active reign in Christ, what will "repentance" mean? How does this view of repentance differ from other commonly-held views?
2. What are the "false lords" and "rival sovereignties" which must be renounced?
3. In what way is God's call to "repent and believe" a continuing call in the Christian life?
4. What resources are given to Christians for living and confessing their new allegiance?

God Accompanies Evangelism with the Signs of His Reign

Remember King Peter of Yugoslavia and King Farouk of Egypt? In the mid-1950s they were royally received at the homes of the titled and the wealthy in Europe. By that time, however, both were ex-monarchs; their titles were meaningless. King Peter had ruled his country for only a few weeks in the early 1940s, and King Farouk, after holding power for 16 years, had been sent into exile by the Egyptian military. Royal dignity and excellence were proclaimed in the titles which each retained, but their homelands now saw in them no signs of royal power.

In contrast, the proclamation of God's kingship in Christ is accompanied by mighty evidences of his reign. Not only did Jesus and his apostles announce this saving rule, but "God also bore witness by signs and wonders and various miracles and by gifts of the Holy Spirit distributed according to his own will" (Heb. 2.3, 4).

The ministry of Jesus himself consisted both of proclaiming the kingdom and performing marvelous signs which pointed to it. On Pentecost Peter spoke of him as "a man attested to you by God with mighty works and wonders and signs which God did through him in your midst" (Acts 2.22). Matthew describes Jesus' ministry in Galilee as one in which he went about "teaching in their synagogues and preaching the gospel of the kingdom and healing every disease and every infirmity among the people" (Matt. 4.23).

Jesus called attention to this two-fold character of his ministry when we read these words from Isaiah (see Isaiah 61.1, 2a) in the synagogue at Nazareth:

> The Spirit of the Lord is upon me,
> because he has anointed me to preach good news to the poor.
> He has sent me to proclaim release to the captives
> and recovering of sight to the blind,
> to set at liberty those who are oppressed,
> to proclaim the acceptance year of the Lord.
> (Luke 4.18, 19)

Immediately he added, "Today this scripture has been fulfilled in your hearing" (Luke 4.21). In like manner, when John the Baptist sent some of his disciples to ask whether Jesus was the awaited Messiah, our Lord replied, "The blind receive their sight and the lame walk, lepers are cleansed and the deaf hear, and the dead are raised up, and the poor have good news preached to them" (Matt. 11.5).

In these passages the acts of deliverance and restoration are distinguished from that of proclaiming the good news, yet they occur along with it. Preaching and signs are distinct, yet intimately connected with each other.

This close connection is also seen in the ministry of the apostles. Evangelizing does not stand alone as though it were merely human verbiage. It is accompanied by the signs of God's reign. In the temple Peter and John heal a lame man in the name of Jesus, and this mighty work occasions further testimony to Messiah's rule (Acts 3). Here a miracle prepares the way for proclamation. At other times the sign of power directly attends the word, as when the Holy Spirit fell upon the household of Cornelius while Peter was proclaiming the good news (Acts 10.34-48). Again, signs of the kingdom power sometimes occur after the message has been given, as proof that what has been spoken has indeed come from God. At Ephesus, for example, God confirmed the word of witness by working "extraordinary miracles by the hands of Paul" (Acts 19.11).

The most characteristic sign to accompany the proclamation of the gospel is the radical change which God effects in those who hear. Paul challenges the Corinthians to test the message of his opponents to see if it is accompanied by power. "For the kingdom of God" he writes, "does not consist in talk but in power" (1 Cor. 4.20). What Paul has in mind is clear from what he writes to the Thessalonians. He recalls that the gospel of the kingdom came to them "not only in word, but also in power, and in the Holy Spirit and with full conviction" (1 Thess. 1.5). That power had been dramatically effective in their lives, for they had "turned to God from idols, to serve a living and true God" (1 Thess. 1.9).

The record is clear. According to his purpose, God bestows his Spirit and works the wonders of rebirth and conversion as the gospel of the kingdom is proclaimed. (See, for example, Acts 13.48; 14.21; 15.7-9; 16.14.) Thus, the Church which the gospel creates is a sign of God's rule. Her faith and works testify to his saving power. After telling the Ephesians that they have been saved by grace through faith and that this is not their own doing, but God's gift, Paul points to God's larger purpose: their lives are now to bear much fruit. "For we are his workmanship, created in Christ Jesus for good works, which God prepared beforehand, that we should walk in them" (Eph. 2.10).

God's wonder-working power, of course, is not limited to the ministry and action of his people. "He does according to his will in the host of heaven and among the inhabitants of the earth (Dan. 4.35). But he is pleased to use Christians to manifest his kingdom in servant ministry as well as in word. As people of the Messiah, the Church is endowed with the Holy Spirit and called to witness to Christ in all of life (Acts 1.8). Her works of mercy and power are to be signs of the kingdom's presence. Transformed by the word of Christ and the work of the Spirit, the Church not only proclaims the gospel, but toils and prays, serves and struggles, that all may know the full blessing of God's reign.

Are our churches today channels for God's transforming work as well as for his saving word? Can even our proclamation be authentic if it does not spring from love—from concern for the total well-being of those who hear us? They evangelize best who also yield themselves to God's service and become sign-bearers of his kingdom. They win converts one by one, but they also manifest God's reign in the wider corporate structures of our world. In apostolic fashion, they put their lives on the line when they preach. What is required of us, then, if we are to be faithful evangelists? At least this: that we show ourselves, in Paul's words, "ready to share . . . not only the gospel of God but also our own selves" (1 Thess. 2.8).

Questions on "God Accompanies Evangelism with the Signs of His Reign"

1. What evidence of God's saving reign should we look for when the gospel is truly proclaimed?
2. In your own congregation, what "signs of the kingdom" can you identify?
3. In what sense are Christian ministries of famine relief, medical care and education "signs of the kingdom"? How are these related to evangelism?
4. Discuss and evaluate these two points of view:
   A. "Leave the social ministries to the humanitarians and the liberals. Our one task is to preach the gospel."
   B. "The time has come for the church to stop talking and get on the forefront in contemporary movements for human liberation."

The Kingdom Imperative: Make Disciples

If you've come with us this far, you know that we've been trying in this series of articles to see evangelism in the light of the kingdom of God. We've been exploring with you what our joint committee's document, *An Evangelism Manifesto*, can mean for the life and work of our churches.

Let's recall the journey we've taken. We began by affirming that *the kingdom of God*—his saving reign in Jesus Christ—*is the central theme of the Bible.* Next we saw that *to evangelize is to proclaim the good news of that kingdom*—"Jesus is Lord." *Evangelism,* accordingly, *always includes the call to submit to God's rule*—to repent and believe the gospel. But we noted also that the work of proclamation does not stand alone. *God accompanies evangelism with the signs of his reign.*

In this final article, we focus on what might be called "the royal command": Christ sends his church to *make disciples* of all nations. We begin to understand the absolute priority of this assignment when we recognize it as (1) the climax and conclusion of the gospels, (2) the central command of the king and (3) the context and condition of his continuing presence with the Church.

Each of the Gospels ends with some form of "the great commission," but it is Matthew who especially emphasizes its climactic character. He, like the other gospel writers, assigns prominence in his narrative to the events surrounding Jesus' death and resurrection. Eight of the 28 chapters deal with those few days. But it is striking to note how Matthew's account points beyond the resurrection. He quotes Jesus as saying on the night of his betrayal, "You will all fall away because of me this night; for it is written, 'I will strike the shepherd, and the sheep of the flock will be scattered.' But after

I am raised up," he continues, "I will go before you to Galilee" (Matt. 28.31, 32). The reader is alerted here to a significant post-resurrection event—the reunion of Jesus with his disciples in Galilee.

When Mary Magdalene and the other Mary first hear the glad news on Easter morning, they are charged to tell the disciples that Jesus is risen and that he is going before them to Galilee. Then, running breathlessly on this errand, they meet the risen Lord himself. "Do not be afraid," he says, "Go and tell my brethren to go to Galilee, and there they will see me" (Matt. 28.10).

Impressive, isn't it—this repeated reference to Galilee? In each instance attention is shifted from the event of the resurrection to the meeting which will follow it. Thus the movement of this gospel, the dramatic buildup of its narrative, is toward that mountain in Galilee. Matthew seems to say, "You haven't understood the purpose of all these things until you know what happened when Jesus met his followers." In this "kingdom gospel" the royal charge to "make disciples" crowns the miracle of Easter.

It is indeed a "royal" command. Jesus introduces it with the staggering claim of universal dominion. "All authority in heaven and on earth has been given to me" (Matt. 28.18). Authority is a key word in this gospel. Matthew tells us how Jesus' teaching was characterized by that note: "He taught us as one who had authority, and not as their scribes" (Matt. 7.29). He stilled the raging waters and banished a host of demons by his word of command. Without hesitation he exercised the divine right of forgiving sins. Hints of his authority thus has appeared here and there throughout his ministry. Now the risen Lord unveils to his followers the full extent of his reign. God has given him everything in the universe to do with as he wills!

Pause to reflect on that for a moment. The kingship of Jesus is not merely a doctrine. It is a fact. God has made him Lord and Christ. The one whom we crucified, he exalted. Our knowledge or ignorance of that, our approval or disapproval, faith or unbelief does not change it in the least. God hasn't merely nominated him as king, subject to our endorsement! He *reigns*, and shall reign until all his enemies are beneath his feet, until every knee shall bow before him, and every tongue confess that Jesus Christ is Lord.

But here the claim of Jesus is the prelude to his commission. He speaks as the one with absolute right to command. He has won the hearts of his followers by his self-giving love and now binds them to his sovereign will. He says in effect, "By the authority committed to me, I send you to make disciples."

But wait—isn't there more to his commission than that? It sounds at first reading like four duties: go, make disciples, baptize and teach. But that perception can be misleading. There is only one imperative verb in the entire sentence, one direct command: "make disciples." The others are participles, surrounding and supporting the imperative. They point to necessary activities that will precede and follow the central task. There is no doubt, however, that the chief calling which the risen king gave to his church in Galilee was to "make disciples of all the nations" (Matt. 28.19).

Further, it is in fulfillment of this task that his followers are to know the joy of his abiding presence. The great commission is the context of his promise, "Lo, I am with you always, to the close of the age" (Matt. 28.20). For this grand purpose he will later send to them his own Spirit. "You shall receive power when the Holy Spirit has come upon you; and you shall be my witnesses in Jerusalem and in all Judea and Samaria and to the end of the earth" (Acts 1.8).

And is there not a sense also in which the missionary obedience of the church is the *condition* of his presence? Has not Jesus promised to abide with and manifest himself to those who keep his commands (John 14.21, 23)? Martin Buber speaks of a deep, underlying principle at work here: "God remains present to you when you have been sent forth; he who goes on a mission has always God before him; the truer the fulfillment, the stronger and more constant his nearness."

And for the church, this present nearness of Christ is more than companionship for the journey—precious as that is. It is also our certain hope of success. Jesus says to his disciples at the outset, "Follow me, and I will make you fishers of men" (Matt. 4.19). He will make them sufficient. He will create their ministry. Remember how he pictured that miracle for them again and again in vivid, unforgettable ways? Peter has been fishing for hours without success. Jesus tells him to launch out into the deep, or put down his nets on the other side of the boat. A puzzled Peter complies, and then the catch swamps him! What he cannot do by himself, at the word of Jesus he *does*.

Again, the hungry multitudes need to be fed, and the disciples have little more than a snack among them. But at his word, they bring their meager fare to Jesus. He blesses it, breaks it, gives it back to them and suddenly there is bread for everyone! When they put their small resources in his hands, he gives them a great ministry. "Lo, I am with you always" (Matt. 28.20). That means that he, the King, is mighty in their midst. How can their labor ever be in vain?

Just what is it now that Christ leads his servants forth to do? What does it mean to "make disciples"? We've learned, to our sadness, that it is more than exporting the glitter and decadence of Western culture. And surely it is more than attaching people to a particular denomination or a sectarian point of view. A disciple, in the New Testament sense of the word, is one who is called into a personal attachment to Jesus in which he trusts, obeys and is transformed by the risen Lord. His disciples thus become his witnesses.

How are we, as agents of the King, to create such people? How can we in our time, "make disciples"? There is no more urgent question for the Church. Here are three dimensions of the answer: by living in genuine community, by pursuing love and justice in the world, and by proclaiming the gospel through every available means.

The church "makes disciples" by living in genuine community. The life of a Christian congregation is meant to illustrate the saving rule of God among men. The new fellowship of redeemed people is one of the chief fruits of his reign. Here forgiveness, acceptance, burden-bearing, and lowly servanthood are to become visible. Here the shared joy of the kingdom is to set a wistful world wondering. Jesus pointed to the magnetic power of a caring community when he said, "By this all men will know that you are my disciples, if you have love for one another" (John 13.35).

Christians "make disciples" also by pursuing love and justice in the world. "Let your light so shine before men," counsels Jesus, "that they may see your good works and give glory to your Father, who is in heaven" (Matt. 5.16). In the good works of his people, God's gracious rule is demonstrated. In our ministry to the world's need, in our struggle for human rights, we are to make winsomely evident the calling and the cost of following Jesus. How will we ever disciple people to him if they cannot see that we are on his side—loving what he loves, hating what he hates, helping what he helps, fighting what he fights—all in his name?

But as we learn to love one another and to serve our generation, let us be urgent also in proclaiming Christ! At all times, by all means, among all peoples, let us share the royal gospel! He is the hope of all the world—Lord and life giver, Savior from sin, deliverer from the coming wrath. But though the Christian message is marvelously redemptive, it will never transform those who have not heard it. If the peoples of the world are ever to become the disciples of Jesus, they must hear his gracious call in the gospel.

Michael Green describes the motivation of the first Christian disciple-makers in these words, "They had an unquenchable conviction that Jesus was the key to life and death, happiness and purpose, and they simply could not keep quiet about him." May it be so for us!

Questions on "The Kingdom Imperative: Make Disciples"

1. As we face our missionary task, what difference should it make to us that Jesus has been given "all authority"?

2. What is the connection between Jesus' promise "Lo, I am with you always" and the miracle of Pentecost?

3. What does it mean to be a "disciple of Jesus"?

4. Why is the mutual love of Christians so strategically important for effective evangelism?

5. What do you plan to do in your congregation about "making disciples of all nations"?

Appendix C
Shopping for God

Kenneth Briggs

For decades now, the baby boom has loomed as a curious aberration and a brute fact that has shaped every major aspect of American life. The baby boomers constitute the largest generation of newborns ever produced in this country, and they have profoundly changed the ways we live and think.

The baby boom began after World War II, when the birthrate suddenly soared, cresting in the late fifties. But the momentum and the extra demand on child-care facilities extended into the sixties.

The bulge was enormous. Between 1945 and 1965, about 75 million infants were added to the citizenship rolls. Meeting their needs meant revamping whole systems. As they grew up, we are told by the experts, their whims and yearnings dominated everything, driving the engine of our holiest of institutions—the marketplace.

This was the generation renowned for responding in surprising, even rebellious, ways to the tumultuous upheavals in the world around it. They sometimes seemed like aliens in their own land, products of their own counterculture. Their strangeness alone qualified them as irresistible research subjects.

Meanwhile, this celebrated generation continues to inch along the mortal life cycle—most, as field reports tell us, settling down to conventional careers and families. But they are leaving their unmistakable mark on society.

Kenneth A. Briggs was religion editor of the *New York Times* from 1974 to 1985 and is now a free-lance writer. This article was originally prepared for *Progressions* and is used with permission.

Appendix C is from the *Church Herald*, April 1991, pp. 8-17. Used by permission.

A Self-Help Movement

Among other things, the baby boomers have spawned a burgeoning self-help movement that includes a thriving trade in therapy and spirituality. They have fostered feminism, accepted higher divorce rates, and demanded better education.

This generation has patronized those distinct enterprises that reflect their tastes: among them, health clubs, condos, and ethnic restaurants. Their imprint on the cultural and economic landscape has been indelible. They are members of what sociologists call the lead generation—so as the boomers go, so goes the nation.

Their influence applies, of course, to religion, where their participation or lack thereof counts heavily. And there we find ambivalence and indifference—attitudes that have church leaders worried and sociologists investigating.

Religious behavior has long been supposed by sociologists to follow an ingrained routine something like this: Children went to church with their parents, absorbed the particular brand of Christianity offered there, avoided church while sowing wild oats during their late teens and twenties, then married, sobered up, had a family and, having returned to their senses, came back to church with their little ones in tow.

Many baby boomers followed that scenario to a T—up to and including the youthful rebellion part. But large numbers of them apparently abandoned the script there; they haven't come back—yet. And many specialists have gone scurrying for explanations.

Among the churches suffering the most serious repercussions of this large-scale absence have been the liberal and moderate mainline denominations. Those churches stood to gain much by the return of those who had attended as youngsters because mainline bodies, more than conservative churches, have depended on their own members' children to replenish their ranks. The mainline churches have been deprived of a rich harvest.

Seeking the Answers

While the churches of the mainstream have been asking what has caused their congregations to become so gray and their numbers to shrink so drastically, survey teams have started looking for answers.

Probing the baby boomers for clues invariably leads to the values and habits that make them distinct. What traits do they exhibit?

Professors Wade Clark Roof of the University of Massachusetts and William McKinney of Hartford Seminary identify several distinguishing marks in their book, *American Mainline Religion: Its Changing Shape and Future*. Among the most valued traits they found were desires for personal freedom and individual fulfillment.

Two important descriptions have also stuck to the generation. It is the first reared by television, and it is the best-educated ever. The range of choices available to boomers was unlike that set before any of their forebears. Many broke with the religious and cultural teachings that had been passed on to them. They became known as a generation that did its own thing.

"Probably more than for any other generation," write Roof and McKinney, "principles of choice and pluralism are accepted as a part of the scheme of things. This alone makes the baby boomers crucial carriers of new values and outlook in contemporary American society."

Evidence about how this preference for choice and mood of non-conformity have affected churchgoing is starting to come in. Some preliminary findings from a survey by Roof paint bold and telling strokes.

Results from 1,400 baby-boomer telephone interviews show that 41 percent have remained connected to the church, 21 percent have returned after dropping out, and one-third (34 percent) have dropped out and stayed out. (The relatively low rate of staying in the church and high rate of staying out are apparent when these figures are compared with those of a similar survey—one that includes other age groups.)

Other evidence in Roof's survey underscores the strong tendency among boomers to separate faith from church. Asked whether it is possible to be a good Christian without going to church, 95 percent of the dropouts said it is. Nearly two-thirds (63 percent) of the dropouts do consider themselves good Christians, compared with 91 percent of the loyalists.

The most encouraging finding of the survey is confirmation of widespread reports of a return to the churches by a modest number of baby boomers.

Still more research is needed to uncover the reasons why many left and others are coming back. But several social scientists are constructing intriguing theories drawn from growing anecdotal material and studies of the generation as a whole.

In general, the boomers are seen as consumers looking to get something specific from a church, should they choose to join one. They are fussier (or more discriminating) than were their parents and will shop around to find the preacher, the spiritual atmosphere, or the church school believed to fulfill their needs. They are—by general agreement of those who study them—not only picky, but highly pragmatic.

Those who go back to church look for two things in particular: religious education for their children and some kind of religious experience that helps make sense of their own lives.

Congregations attentive to "young-adult themes," Roof says, "are showing lots of ferment." Some migrate toward conservative evangelical churches and others toward mainline churches that strike some kind of balance between the religion the boomers knew as children and the attention to issues that concern them now.

Recapturing the Fifties

"Many come back with images from the fifties of what religion should feel like," says professor David Roozen of Hartford Seminary. "The images come from their days as kids with their families in worship and Sunday school. Sometimes they move into evangelical churches that are most like [those of] the fifties, or into the mainline ones that blend that [style] with contemporary overlays."

A common shift among the baby boomers, Roozen says, is from belief in specific Christian doctrines or fundamentals to a more amorphous spirituality. Some shop for a church that will fill that need. In the Roof survey, one in five (20 percent) boomers said they had attended a "spiritual-growth seminar."

As the avenues for religious and spiritual exploration have multiplied, Roozen says, many baby boomers appear to do their own searching privately, availing themselves of the myriad resources of bookstores, television, and a host of therapies and self-help centers.

Marriage and Children

Marriage and children, both of which baby boomers have tended to postpone, may provide some with a reason to return to church—especially if those life changes are accompanied by a swing toward traditional values.

"Parenting gives people incentive," Roozen says. "People want help. They find it's not easy to be a parent, especially if they've spent fifteen years being free and single. They may be reassessing their own values toward more tradition, and it makes sense for them to go to an institution that identifies itself with tradition."

Among the most urgent questions for mainline churches is what trends among the returnees indicate for the denominations' efforts to regain momentum. As Roof begins assessing survey data, he says the patterns are not yet clear.

"Many are going to conservative churches and many are not," he says. "What impresses me is that many of these people are looking for faith that is related to the modern world. I think there's a new interest in resurrecting the old church around young adults who are juggling family, marriage, and careers." But, he adds, the proportion returning overall is probably not as high as that of previous generations.

For every boomer who feels the itch to seek out a suitable congregation, obviously another—at least—does not. As the survey findings show, the dropouts seem more numerous in highly urban, trend-setting states. Whatever their interest in ruminating over religious questions, they do not, for whatever reason, feel that the church is a necessary part of that quest.

'Returnees' Vs. 'Dropouts'

The split into "returnees" and "dropouts" could portend a widening gulf between a community of churched people with traditional views and a growing minority of unchurched people with unconventional beliefs.

"The differences between the churched and the unchurched along the lines of liberal and conservative attitudes is growing," Roozen says. "It has increased, and I suspect it will [continue to] increase."

Research results in the next year or two should provide more information about the directions the baby boomers are taking—including the nature and extent of the shift that is leading some of them toward churches again.

Where a Generation Hungers

Robert Bast

Understanding people is the necessary first step in being able to minister to them. I have chosen to separate three primary areas of need from the list of issues and concerns of the baby boom generation. I do so for two reasons. First, because a case can be made that the needs which will be discussed here are, in fact, the issues of greatest concern and significance to this generation. Second, because they are the needs to which the church can respond and, through responding, provide the greatest likelihood of connecting. By connecting, I mean not simply gaining a hearing, but making a difference. These are the hungers for which the church can provide bread.

A Longing for Spiritual Reality

Anyone who spends time listening to baby boomers will probably hear evidence of dissatisfaction, perhaps even of emptiness. *Wistfulness* is the term Paul Light has used to describe this pattern. The word means characterized by unfulfilled longing or desire. It conveys a sense of pathos, a feeling of sorrow that what one has longed for may not be found. The great expectations of the baby boomers make them particularly vulnerable to disappointment. However, here we focus not so much on unfulfilled dreams as on unfulfilled lives.

It is not difficult to document the sense of a basic lack, an empty core, in the lives of many baby boomers. One can see it all around in our culture, including in books and films. That emptiness, of course, is not unique to baby boomers. It has been present since people were old enough to understand their feelings. What is more recent is the recognition that what is longed for has not been found

---

The late Rev. Robert L. Bast was minister for evangelism and church development for the Reformed Church in America. This article is excerpted from his book *The Missing Generation: The Church's Ministry with the Baby Boom* published by Reformed Church Press and available through the RCA Distribution Center, (800) 688-7221.

where people have been looking, and that the search has been going on long enough to show it isn't fruitful.

For all their celebration of freedom and pursuit of material gain, members of the baby boom generation have awakened to the fact that they have come up empty. What is significant is that this is being recognized and acknowledged, especially by those who have managed to carve out the largest slice of the pie.

American Demographics magazine recently featured an article on the New Age movement. A major focus of the article was an emphasis on the type of people who are responding to New Age thinking. "Affluent baby boomers are the group most likely to embrace the so-called New Age movement." In analyzing the appeal to "educated, affluent, successful people," the author came up with this reason: "They are hungry for something that mainstream society has not given them. They say they are looking for 'alternatives,' 'new paradigms,' 'social transformation,' 'personal wholeness,' 'enlightenment,' and even 'utopia'."

The article goes on to cite a survey that estimates that the New Age movement has approximately 11.5 million serious adherents, and with the recent popularizing of the movement "that figure is probably a good deal larger." I can hardly imagine those figures are accurate. Still, we may well be awed by the massive success of the New Age movement.

Now the reasons for New Age success. We have quoted the explanation given by the author, which suggests that it is primarily a sense of inner emptiness, a wistful longing, or a spiritual quest that has led people into New Age. One person quoted in the article was more specific, pointing out that those in the New Age movement "don't care for existing religions, so they have come out with a new kind of religion—a New Age one, a kind of attunement."

We do well to give attention to what this person is saying and not to underestimate the fervor with which existing religions are being rejected. It will not be easy to surmount this attitude. Institutions do not change readily, and the church is no exception. Major changes will be required in congregations if they are to have an effective ministry.

It intrigues me that this article in such a cutting edge magazine places such stress on the status of the New Age clientele. In this short article, I counted twenty-four references to their social standing: affluent (4); high income (5); highly educated (6); successful (2); professional (2); discriminating (2); world travelers (1); creative (1); and trendsetters (1). Obviously, someone is eager to point out that the followers of New Age are the elite, the cream of the crop.

If anyone could find fulfillment in what the world has to offer, these people should be expected to have found it. All the commonly accepted avenues to fulfillment were open to them: education, money, travel, success, status. Yet they are still searching.

In its closing paragraph, the article raises a question about the future of New Age. "It's possible that the recent boom in New Age interest will turn out to be a fad fueled by bored, restless baby boomers." The author discounts that possibility. None of us has any idea how long the New Age movement will be popular. What we do know is that the basic spiritual hunger which has led many people into New Age will continue as long as people persist in looking for fulfillment where it cannot be found.

The spiritual hunger of the baby boomer is identified by other observers. John Naisbitt, in *Megatrends 2000*, suggests that America is probably on the verge of a major religious awakening or revival. In 1985, Craig Dykstra, then at Princeton Theological Seminary, wrote a thought-provoking editorial in *Theology Today* in which he raises the possibility that we may be on the threshold of a religious awakening. Dykstra quotes John Wheeler, introduced as president of the Center for the Vietnam Generation, who says: "Questions of faith and spirit have emerged strongly at the close of this decade [especially] among that cohort of the population we call the baby boomers." Wheeler gives three reasons: First, the baby boom generation has faced and remembers death. Second, this is a time of reevaluation for many, a time of asking what all the striving and acquiring finally amount to, and what really does have value. Wheeler points out that material security and self-concern do not save us from a sense of spiritual void. Third, Wheeler mentions science, "which, though it gives us no final answers, drives us to metaphors reminiscent of Genesis."

Against this background, Dykstra raises questions about how the church will respond to this longing for spiritual fulfillment that is going on around it. He suggests that those who approach the church in their search will probably do so with some hesitation. In light of the common baby boom attitude of distrust for religious institutions, Dykstra is surely right. He is also right, I believe, in identifying that which those who do approach the church are truly seeking:

> The deepest question they are asking—and may not yet dare to ask out loud—is this: Do you know God? If they sense we do not, again they will go away—perhaps this time more sadly than cynically. And if they sense we do, it will not be because we *say* we do. It will be because they see it in the way we live, in the manner of our speaking, and in our willingness to listen and to search. They will see it in the freedom this knowledge provides, and in what this knowledge commits us to.

Yes. If there is one thing the world has a right to expect of the church, it is the knowledge of God. That God can be known because

God has made himself known, that we know him because he has found us, and that we will open our lives and our churches so that others who hunger for God may be satisfied. That is what we want to help pilgrims understand and believe.

A Hunger for Community

Community is the second great need evident in baby boomers, and again it is one to which the church is surely able to respond. The hunger for community is frequently identified as an important concern of this generation. Daniel Yankelovich speaks of this at some length. "A hunger for deeper personal relationships shows up in our research findings as a growing concern. . . . [Our] surveys show that 70 percent of Americans now recognize that while they have many acquaintances they have few close friends—and they experience this as a serious void in their lives."

The absence of community not only produces loneliness, which is a common enough problem, but also gives rise to deeper distress. The absence of community, says Yankelovich, "is experienced as an aching loss, a void, a sense of homelessness. The symptoms of its absence are feelings of isolation, falseness, instability, and impoverishment of spirit."

But what is community? Yankelovich points out that while it is not easy to define the term, it can be understood by the feelings it evokes, such as: "Here is where I belong, these are my people, I care for them, they care for me, I am part of them, I know what they expect from me and I from them, they share my concerns, I know this place, I am on familiar ground, I am at home."

The United Methodist Church held a conference on the theme "Reaching for the Baby Boomer." One of the features was a panel made up of young adults. Someone asked one of the women a question about what community meant to her. She said, "Community is being there for each other when we have a need, or are needed. Relationships are very important to me, and must be characterized by loyalty and commitment. I value acceptance of me as I am, the honesty which lets me be myself, the feeling that we can disagree without harming the relationship. That is community."

We live in a society in which that kind of community is hard to come by. Many young adults struggle with commitment. In their busy lives, relationships tend to be formed primarily in the workplace, and time and circumstances make it difficult for such relationships to move beyond superficiality. Community is dependent on an ongoing and time-consuming process, and many people are too busy to engage in it.

Beyond reasons of time lies a deeper problem—our struggle for intimacy. Often that word is used in a sexual context, but of course it is much broader and richer than that. Intimacy has to do with relationships which are close, lasting, and personal, in which people are known to one another as they truly are, and relate in genuineness and depth.

An article on intimacy appeared recently in the *Chicago Tribune*. The author points out that "when we talk about intimacy, we're talking about being able to share our inmost self with someone else, and having that sharing reciprocated." While that is what many people would like, most do not know how—or where—to find it. The article quotes a professor of psychology who has written a book on intimacy: "Today, intimacy is harder for us, so we're more preoccupied with it. What I hear is a feeling of resignation. People realize they're not finding the fulfillment they had hoped to find."

Robert Gribbon has done extensive research on baby boomers and their relationship with the church. His research points out that the desire for intimacy is a prime factor in bringing baby boomers back to church. "Those seeking the church are working primarily on the life issue of intimacy." In his interviews with returnees, Gribbon noted "the overwhelming emphasis on belonging," and indicated that those turning to the church are looking for "friends, for a community of shared value, for support with life tasks, and a personalized but structured relationship with ultimate reality."

Here then is a need which the church is uniquely suited to address. The message of our faith is of a God who absolutely and unconditionally accepts us, and whose challenge to the faith community is, "Just as I have loved you, you also should love one another" (John 13.34). At its best, the church is the home and family for which people are searching. True community can be found here and it exists, not just for those who now experience it, but for all whose hearts hunger for home.

Support with Life Tasks

Gribbon's research identified the desire to obtain support for life tasks as another important factor leading people in the baby boom generation to turn to the church.

Many baby boomers live apart from an immediate or extended family. Even where distance is not a factor, changes in lifestyles have weakened relationships with other relatives and the amount of time spent with them is considerably less than it was in earlier eras. As a result, many feel they have no one to share in their struggle with life tasks.

Cheryl Russell identifies four primary life tasks in the lives of baby boomers: home, marriage, family, and work. She predicts that home and family concerns will dominate in the foreseeable future. "Because of the middle-aging of the baby boom, the United States is about to become a nation of homebodies. . . . For the next two decades, the home will be the focus of American life, like it was in the 1950s." Family themes will be high on the agenda.

In another study, Robert Gribbon looked at people in their thirties and explored issues to which the church could respond. Gribbon found that the day-to-day tasks of managing, parenting, and householding were a major concern for them. "Dissatisfaction with one's income, marriage, and parents tends to be greatest in the thirties," he noted. This may give rise to a search for self-improvement.

While not the primary reason people seek the church, it is a factor. It has long been true that the arrival and rearing of children leads people to think about imparting values and providing religious training for children. One of the people Gribbon interviewed said, "I came for the sake of the children, but I found something for myself." Gribbon cites Hoge's study of Roman Catholic converts, which found "the religious instruction of children was a motivating factor for 45 percent of those who sought the church." Gribbon points out that people "may come to church for the sake of the children, but they don't stay for the sake of the children."

It is often a personal need for support which both attracts and involves people in the church. Life is complicated, and the need for encouragement and support is being increasingly recognized. A participant in a baby boom panel expressed the view of many when she indicated that she goes to church to find help in coping with the pressures of the week. "I go to church on Sunday," she said, "to find strength to get to Friday."

The Legacy of the Baby Boom

"The Legacy of the Baby Boom" is the title of the concluding chapter in Landon Jones's classic work, *Great Expectations*. Jones can guide us in a brief look at some elements in the baby boom that are likely to endure:

- This is a generation that has always seen itself as unique, and can be understood as a generational unit.
- This is a generation that was once united in its conviction that it has a mission to develop fulfillment and harmony and to create wholeness in people. Now it is moving from optimism to pessimism.
- This is a generation that grew up with unrealistic and unachievable expectations. Now it has bumped up against limits. "They had expected to be the masters of change, but now change has mastered them," writes Landon Jones.
- This is a generation that has helped create skepticism that challenges all our institutions and values. Now authority is everywhere in decline, and all truth is relative.

- This is a generation that has redefined the family norm and allowed for the acceptance of a host of different lifestyles.

For better or worse, the baby boomers have changed American society: in many ways permanently. They have brought new freedoms, created new opportunities for women, raised the level of concern for the environment, contributed to the cause of world peace, reduced discrimination, lifted standards of excellence, stressed education, and made us more tolerant. They have also helped make our society more materialistic and self-centered, more skeptical and fragmented.

For all the changes they have created in society, they have had far less success in changing themselves. That is both a reason for disappointment and a source of hope. After all, they are still searching.

Opening Doors

James Lankheet

"We don't want anything fundamental and right-wing," said a couple coming back to church after years away. "We want openness. We want to come back, but we need to take it slow."

"Now that our child is growing up, coming to church is important to me," said another woman.

"I attended Sunday school for years at a church when I was young," said the single young man who was engaged to be married. "I just thought it was time to get back with a church."

"I tried to get to church for the past four months," said the single parent, "but I only made it this past week. I am not sure how involved I will be in this church, but I do plan on attending now and then."

All of these people want something from their church. They want openness. They want a church that will embrace the concerns of families, of married people, of seekers in the faith. And they are unashamed about wanting what they want in a church.

Young adults born between the years of 1946 and 1964 compose a generation with distinct values, attitudes, and outlooks on the world. They are America's largest (76 million) and noisiest generation. Who they are as a generation to a great extent determines what they want in a church.

The identity of boomers and their impact on society has changed with the times. Landon Y. Jones, in his book *Great Expectations: America and the Baby Boom Generation*, says that the generation made the fifties the era of the schools, the sixties the age of protest, the seventies the Me Decade, and the eighties a times of obsession with jobs, homes, and children. Mass marketing zeroed in on this generation as early as the fifties and sixties. The market sold them "Howdy-Doody," then Pepsi. Today it's "thirtysomething" and Diet Pepsi.

The church has responded to their needs, too. Strong Sunday school programs in the fifties and sixties were a response to a generation turning school-aged. Singles ministries in churches rose and fell as the population bulge moved through the seventies. The eighties brought a desire for contemporary music in worship, practical preaching, and strong Christian education for children.

The Rev. James K. Lankheet is pastor of West Broward Community Church in Sunrise, Florida.

Yet as the nineties begin, this generation is noticeably smaller and quieter in most churches across the nation. The average church member today is fiftyish. Instead of a bulge in the membership of churches, the boomer generation often represents a gap. Will twenty-six-to-forty-year-olds take their place in church next to their parents? We will, they respond, if the church provides what we want.

Openness and Flexibility

This next generation desires an openness in the church community. Boomers ask themselves, is there going to be a place for me at this church, a place for my doubts, my questions, by conclusions, even if they may seem out of line? Many came of age in the free-thinking and questioning 1960s. As a result, boomers (especially those born between 1946 and 1955) desire flexibility and openness in their church.

A thirty-six-year-old father on his way back to church went through the new members' class but stopped short of joining the church. His reason: "I have lots of questions." He wonders how people can really know if the Bible is true. Is there room for his struggle in the community of faith? Another young adult, when asked by a reporter why he no longer goes to church, replied, "Even when the church encourages discussion, it assumes the outcome in advance."

This generation needs a forum for its questions. They need reasons. They ask, "Why should I try the church?" Once they are in the church door, they will ask, "Why should I believe what is being taught here?" If a church does what it does but does not know why and does not encourage questions, it will have a hard time reaching out to the next generation.

This doesn't mean that the church of the nineties should be all questions and no answers. The crucial factor is our openness to questions and to people. Churches and their people will be tempted to mow down questions; questions can be unsettling. Yet God's Word says that the "grass withers, the flower fades; but the word of our God will stand forever" (Isa. 40.8). The promise for those who stand by the Word is that the questions will fade and the Word will stand. Trusting in the Word that stands forever, the church must be open to people and the questions they bring.

The challenge of outreach to boomers is to listen to the questions without quenching the Spirit who may be prompting the questions. Above all, outreach to boomers requires openness to the people behind the questions. To welcome and to walk with people at various stages in their faith journey—that is the goal of outreach.

Loyalties Redefined

Like the single parent who says that she can't commit herself to the church even though she plans on attending now and then, boomers have their own way of understanding loyalty and commitment to the church.

Unlike many of their parents, boomers will not become involved or stay involved in a particular local church for reasons of loyalty alone. A recent report from the Barna Research Group, titled "America 2000: What the Trends Mean for Christianity," noted that more and more people are moving away from having one home congregation. People are connecting with a variety of congregations that are tapped according to need.

But this apparent lack of loyalty to the visible church does not necessarily mean a lack of loyalty to Christ. That reality is a stumbling block to good Calvinists. People from Reformed backgrounds may remember that John Calvin once said that "you cannot have God as your Father unless you have the Church as your Mother." Yet boomers today seem instinctively to resist this. For them a commitment to God and a commitment to the church are hardly the same thing.

Recent surveys show that even though many people say that they believe in Jesus Christ, those same people may have little or no connection to a local church. That's troubling, especially for loyal church members. Yet boomers hardly seem ashamed about it. They reason away their connection to the church by saying they have become disillusioned with it, that the church is irrelevant to the practical issues of their lives, or that it is just too rigid.

Traditional thinking is that if people are committed to Christ, their commitment will result in involvement in a local church. They prove their theory by pointing out how the most committed people are the most involved. They point out how Jesus himself said, "You will know them by their fruits" (Matt. 7.16).

Yet another line of thinking says that as people become involved, they become more committed. Commitment grows as people become more involved. This approach centers on the fact that people will bear fruit when they are connected to the vine and branches (John 15.1-11). No connections, no fruit.

This involvement-producing-commitment approach is best for outreach to boomers. The way to reach boomers is by making lots of connections to the vine and the branches. The more connected a boomer is to the vine, the more fruit. Involvement yields commitment. The more connections to Jesus Christ and his church, the more fruit will be produced.

For boomers, the words *commitment* and *loyalty* need redefinition. For them commitments do not automatically result in involvement. Rather, commitments and loyalties are nurtured and grow as tasks are shared, as needs are met, and as people share their faith journeys. There need to be many open doors in congregations that desire to welcome new people to involvement.

Meet My Needs

Like the woman whose motivation to come back to church is her growing child, boomers arrive at church because they have very specific needs and wants. Some want clean and spacious nurseries for their young children. They want varied and meaningful programs for their older children. They want preaching and teaching that is practical and relevant to their lives. They want social groups that give them a name and a face. They want to belong. They want opportunities for leadership. And they want options—options in worship times and styles, options in their education and growth opportunities, and options in the way that they can use their gifts in the life of the church.

Some churches may be uncomfortable with new people who are so aggressive about what they want in a church. They argue that people should be asking what they can do for the church and not the other way around. But recall Jesus' healing of blind Bartimaeus (Mark 10.46ff). The blind man cries out to Jesus, "Have mercy on me!" Although the crowd tells Bartimaeus to keep quiet, Jesus says, "Call him here." When Bartimaeus stands before Jesus, the Lord asks him, "What do you *want* me to do for you?" He replies, "My teacher, let me see again." Jesus says, "Go; your faith has made you well." And the man was healed.

Likewise, churches need to ask boomers, "What do you *want* us to do for you?" And when they respond with their wants, the church had better follow through.

Outreach Boomer Style

Suppose that Bob and Abbey Vine, who are active members of their local church, want to reach out to their neighbors, Will and Mary Graft. The Vines have invited the Grafts to come to church with them, but the Grafts say that they usually spend Sundays with Will's daughter, whom he only can see on Sundays.

The Vines are at a loss for how to proceed in their outreach to the Grafts. Although their neighbors have a basic knowledge of the Christian faith, they seem unwilling to adjust their schedule to attend church.

Wanting to give up but believing in the importance of outreach, the Vines decide to commit the Grafts to prayer. They ask God for direction in how to continue their outreach to them. Then one day Abbey notices that Mary seems isolated while caring for her two-year-old son at home. Seeing this need, Abbey invites Mary to come with her to the church's MOMS ministry, a Bible study and support group for mothers that meets Tuesday mornings at the church while nursery care is provided.

After three weeks, Mary is beginning to feel comfortable in the group. Then one evening she suggests to her husband that "maybe we should go to Bob and Abbey's church this Sunday. I am finding that it is a really friendly place. Besides, I think it is important for our son as he grows up."

Meanwhile, Bob has invited Will to the Christian business luncheon. The discussions there have stimulated Will's spirituality and he also has been thinking about attending a church. The next Sunday, Will and Mary Graft and their young son attend church together for the first time.

This begins the Grafts' involvement in a loyal church. Through prayer and the leading of God's Spirit, their involvement results in greater faithfulness to Jesus Christ and his church.

The church of the nineties that would minister effectively should develop an openness in its believing community, offer many opportunities for involvement, and offer spiritual programs that meet needs. Through prayer and the blessing of the Holy Spirit, a commitment to work with young adults on their puzzling and complex lives will result in lives that yield to the lordship of Jesus Christ. And that reign of Jesus Christ in the heart of every person must be the goal that beckons us to get busy.

Additional Resources

Abraham, William. *The Logic of Evangelism*. Grand Rapids: Eerdmans, 1989.

Aldrich, Joseph C. *Life-Style Evangelism: Crossing Traditional Boundaries to Reach the Unbelieving World*. Portland: Multnomah, 1981.

Armstrong, Richard S. *The Pastor as Evangelist*. Philadelphia: Westminster, 1984.

Augsburger, David W. *Communicating Good News*. Scottdale: Mennonite Publishing House, 1972.

Bast, Robert L. "Evangelism Ideas and Resources" (included in a mailing from the minister for evangelism and church development, Reformed Church in America).

____. "Where a Generation Hungers." The *Church Herald* XLVIII, No. 4 (April 1991), pp. 11-14.

____. *The Missing Generation: The Church's Ministry with the Baby Boom*. Grand Rapids: Reformed Church Press, 1989.

Briggs, Kenneth. "Shopping for God." The *Church Herald* XLVIII, No. 4 (April 1991), pp. 8-10.

Callahan, Kennon. *Twelve Keys to an Effective Church*. New York: Harper & Row, 1983.

____. *Effective Church Leadership: Building on the Twelve Keys*. San Francisco: Harper & Row, 1990.

Conn, Harvie M. *Evangelism: Doing Justice and Preaching Grace*. Grand Rapids: Zondervan, 1982.

Costas, Orlando. *Liberating News: A Theology of Contextual Evangelization*. Grand Rapids: Eerdmans, 1989.

Dale, Robert D. and Delos Miles. *Evangelizing the Hard-To-Reach*. Nashville: Broadman, 1986.

Evangelism in Reformed Perspective: An Evangelism Manifesto. (booklet) Grand Rapids: the *Church Herald* and the *Banner*, 1977.

Guder, Darrell L. *Be My Witnesses*. Grand Rapids: Eerdmans, 1985.

Henderson, Robert T. *Joy to the World: An Introduction to Kingdom Evangelism*. Atlanta: John Knox, 1980.

Hunter, George G., III. *To Spread the Power: Church Growth in the Wesleyan Spirit*. Nashville: Abingdon, 1987.

Johnson, Ben. *An Evangelism Primer: Practical Principles for Congregations*. Atlanta: John Knox, 1983.

Kraft, Charles. *Communication Theory for Christian Witness*. Nashville: Abingdon, 1983.

Krass, Alfred C. *Evangelizing Neo-Pagan North America*. Scottdale: Herald Press, 1982.

Lankheet, James. "Opening Doors." The *Church Herald* XLVIII, No. 4 (April 1991), pp. 15-17.

Mission and Evangelism: An Ecumenical Affirmation—A Study Guide for Congregations. New York: National Council of Churches, 1983.

Newbigin, Lesslie. *The Open Secret*. Grand Rapids: Eerdmans, 1978.

____. *Foolishness to the Greeks*. Grand Rapids: Eerdmans, 1986.

Pippert, Rebecca Manley. *Out of the Saltshaker & Into the World*. Downers Grove: InterVarsity, 1979.

Schaller, Lyle E. *Assimilating New Members*. Nashville: Abingdon, 1978.

____. *Growing Plans*. Nashville: Abingdon, 1983.

____. "How Do You Initiate New Members in the Tribe?" *Church Growth America* (Nov.-Dec. 1979), pp. 8-9.

Van Engen, Charles. "Church Growth, Yes! But Which Kind?" the *Church Herald* (Aug. 5, 1977), pp. 12, 13, 28.

____. "Your Church Cannot Grow—Without the Holy Spirit," the *Church Herald* (Apr. 21, 1978), pp. 6-8.

____. "Let's Contextualize Kingdom Growth," The *Church Herald* (Nov. 3, 1978), pp. 10-12.

____. *God's Missionary People: Rethinking the Purpose of the Local Church*. Grand Rapids: Baker, 1991.

Wagner, Peter. *Leading Your Church to Growth*. Glendale: Regal, 1984.

____. "Concepts of Evangelism Have Changed Over the Years," *Evangelical Missions Quarterly XX*, No. 1 (Jan. 1974), pp. 41-42.

____. *Your Spiritual Gifts Can Help Your Church Grow*. Glendale: Regal, 1974.

Willimon, William H.. *The Gospel for the Person Who Has Everything*. Valley Forge: Judson Press, 1984.

Wuthnow, Robert. "Evangelicals, Liberals, and the Perils of Individualism," *Perspectives* VI:5 (May 1991), pp. 10-13.